Waking Up in America

How One Doctor Brings Hope to

Those Who Need It Most

PEDRO JOSÉ GREER JR., M.D.

with Liz Balmaseda

SIMON & SCHUSTER

SIMON & SCHUSTER
Rockefeller Center
1230 Avenue of the Americas
New York, NY 10020

SIMON & SCHUSTER and colophon are
registered trademarks of Simon & Schuster Inc.

Designed by Ruth Lee

Manufactured in the United States of America

1   3   5   7   9   10   8   6   4   2

Library of Congress Cataloging-in-Publication Data
Greer, Pedro José.
Waking up in America : how one doctor brings hope to those who need
it most / Pedro José Greer Jr. with Liz Balmaseda.
p.   cm.
1. Greer, Pedro José.   2. Missionaries, Medical—Florida—Miami
Metropolitan Area Biography.   3. Homeless persons—Medical care—
Florida—Miami Metropolitan Area.   4. Poor—Medical care—
Florida—Miami Metropolitan Area.   I. Balmaseda, Liz.   II. Title.
R722.32.G734A3   1999
610'.92—dc21   99-30152
[B]   CIP
ISBN 0-684-83547-9

To
my wife, Janus, and my children, Alana and Joey.
Mom, Dad, and Sally.
Tito, you are my brother.
And to you,
Chichi,
peace.

Contents

Waking Up
in America

Introduction

⌐

I STARTED WRITING THIS BOOK IN A
hotel room in San Juan, Puerto Rico, six years ago. I had
just finished giving a lecture entitled "A Physician's Responsibility to the Poor" at an annual medical-student
convention. That lecture had opened up some old, painful
memories and sent me back to files I had not read in a long
while. Over the years, I had kept cryptic notes of my journey into the world of medicine and the sick, the homeless
and the poor, the world of politics, HMOs, and other horrors. I wanted to write in a language that would reach the
students. I wanted to convey my sense of mission. I
wanted to tell them about passion. I wanted to tell them
about the things I had learned, the things they would
never learn in the lab. I wanted to tell about the joy I found
in my profession, particularly when it involved my patients.

I'm a hepatologist and gastroenterologist by formal
training. But I have never had a liver or a colon walk into

my office alone. They always came attached to a person. That person had a family, friends, a history, dreams. As physicians, I told the students, we treat people, not organs or diseases.

So, in the early summer of 1993, in a hotel room overlooking the Caribbean, I began to write my story. My friend Raul Mateu convinced me this was a story that went beyond medicine. He encouraged me to reconstruct my experiences, to pull back the lens and view the larger landscape of my work. So I wrote this book, with my friend Liz Balmaseda, about my years working with Miami's poor and homeless.

As do many of my most vivid memories, this story contains many heartaches. But I believe it is mostly a story of hope, of helping others, of what can be achieved if only we follow our hearts. This book is about the homeless and the sick, and about battling the systems that put them through hell.

When I took the Hippocratic oath, in June 1984, I vowed to protect people against disease, to protect human life, to do everything possible in the name of healing. If that means I have to break rules, so be it. The health of my patient comes first.

As a young doctor, I was inspired beyond my wildest dreams to build a clinic for the homeless, another for undocumented immigrants, and to establish a few other provisional facilities for the poor. In the process, I learned that the beauty of America is this simple: if we find it wrong, we can make it right.

I was born in this country by chance, in the emergency room of Jackson Memorial Hospital, where I would begin my medical internship twenty-eight years later. My mother, almost seven months pregnant, was visiting from Havana that day in 1956. She had come for my grand-father's birthday party—not mine—but began having contractions the night before the party, and hurried to the emergency room.

The intern who treated her told her she was in false labor.

"Don't worry, lady, that's all it is," the intern's supervising resident confidently repeated.

"Hurts like hell for false contractions," my mother replied.

The resident and intern walked away, as if their business had been completed. The resident gave a wink to a passing nurse and remarked:

"HLF. Hysterical Latin female."

"*Idiota!*" my mother whispered.

Less than three hours later, I was born on a gurney in the ER. Amid the chaos that decades later would mark my life as a doctor training in a public hospital, I had woken up in America. Within two weeks I was back in Cuba.

Little did I know I was simply continuing a long tradition in a family of international travelers. It was the British battles against Oliver Cromwell that first brought my ancestors to America. The Civil War destroyed their farm in Georgia. The Spanish-American War took my great-grandfather to Cuba. The Castro revolution brought us back to Miami.

In Cuba we were not a family of means. In fact, my father would say we were one of the few Cuban families who lost nothing to the Castro regime.

"Why?" I'd ask.

"Because we *had* nothing," he would say.

Although I can trace the turning points of my family history by world-impacting events, my life has been defined by the little things, memories of the sixties and seventies, of campus life at the University of Florida. I'm a Cuban-Irish-American guy genetically predisposed to travel between tragedy and conspiracy—and hit every good party along the way.

This book will take you from a high school football game to the political games of Washington, from the universe of the sick to the recesses of homelessness, from the death of a loved one to the life of a homeless child who offers a prophetic message.

Just imagine how different it would be if we judged a little less and listened a little more, if each of us did something, anything, that could help someone else. I hope my story moves you to action, to extend your hand and help a person in need, to right the wrongs. Each of us has the power to change this world.

Peace,

P. J. Greer Jr.

Waking Up
in America

⌒

The Game:

A Miami

Parable,

in Slo-Mo

CHRISTOPHER COLUMBUS BOYS Catholic High School in Miami had the worst football team in Dade County history, perhaps in the history of the world. We were a small ensemble—so small that on the field some of us had to play both ways. (Back then, that meant playing offense and defense.) You could fit the entire team in a midsized Subaru. But we played our hearts out. We won our first game during my junior year, but then managed to go eighteen consecutive games without winning again. Our team was so bad that the priest who led our pregame prayer didn't even mention victory, only pleas for no injuries.

Then came our Homecoming game, and the night the world shifted. It was a warm evening at the Orange Bowl in November 1973, my senior year. We were playing a top-ranked team, Miami High School, the oldest public school in the city. From the start, the game was historic for us: we actually made first downs; we actually made touchdowns. I even made a seventy-three-yard punt. At the end of the second quarter, we filed off the field in utter disbelief—we weren't losing. We were tied.

The third quarter was unremarkable. The only thing memorable about it was that for the first time in two years—seventy-five quarters—we were going into the final quarter with a decent chance of winning.

With two minutes left to go in the game, we were down 13 to 20, and just fifteen yards away from scoring another touchdown. Out in the stands, the urban Cubans of Miami High, better known as Havana High, expressed their true feelings for us, the Americanized suburban Cubans of Columbus High: "¡Arriba, abajo, Columbus pa'l carajo!" (Up, down, Columbus go to hell!).

We drove to the two-yard line, where our fullback took the ball in for an off-tackle touchdown run. With just a minute and thirty-two seconds remaining on the clock, the score was tight: Miami High 20, Columbus 19.

We had just one chance to win the first game since forever. We were going for two. But we were totally unprepared for victory. We had no victory dance. We had no victory cheer. We had no marching band, just five guys stomping around the field at halftime, blowing kazoos. And this time, we had no piddly little starting team across the scrimmage line, either. No, we were facing a real football team, burly Havana High.

In the glare of the stadium lights of the world-famous Orange Bowl, I leaned forward and took my position in the huddle, my arms pressed upon my knees. I heard our quarterback call the play that would define the season: "Tackle eligible." Technically, I was the starting left offensive tackle, and on defense, outside linebacker. But I was about to become a receiver. I could feel the elbow pads slip down my sweat-soaked arms. My heart raced with fear and a mix of thrill and doom as I left the huddle and took my place in the field. I prayed every prayer I knew, English and Spanish. As the ball was snapped, I jumped up to block, shuffled left, and ran toward the end zone.

The rest of the sequence seemed to happen in slow motion. The ball left the quarterback's hand, arched gracefully toward me as I leapt into the air, and slipped safely into my hands. I had jumped up and caught the ball. I caught the ball. With my hands. In the end zone.

I jumped and jumped and jumped in elation. Columbus was ahead, 21 to 20. The game was over. Miami High attempted a field goal, but we blocked the kick. My teammates hoisted me upon their shoulders and carried me off the field. Who could have guessed? A victory had come at last, even against a formidable rival. We tasted heaven, even when the crowd cheered, "Go to hell!" Who would have guessed? There we were, the screwups, the Three Stooges of high school football. But that night, the night the world shifted, we were Homecoming heroes.

I have held the sweetness of that night in my memory ever since. In moments of hopelessness, when the forces seem to line up against any glimmer of victory, it has hoisted me once again in an orange rush of possibility and glided me to a better place, kazoos buzzing triumphantly in my wake.

Never give up.

Waking Up

~

*For every hour and every moment
thousands of men leave life on this earth,
and their souls appear before God. And
how many of them depart in solitude,
unknown, sad, dejected that no one
mourns for them or even knows whether
they have lived or not!*

—Dostoyevsky, *The Brothers Karamazov*

I WAS SURE IT WAS MY OWN EXHAUS-
tion playing tricks on me. It seemed to lift me into that
kind of smiling high as my open red Jeep Wrangler
pressed through the early morning jam on a stretch of the
eastbound expressway on my way to Jackson Memorial

Hospital, some fifteen years ago. In the amber light of the Miami morning, I didn't notice the usual grate of engine noise, the drive-time daredevils who negotiate traffic while shaving or applying mascara, the big city's pockets of chronic inertia. No, not that morning. I had that pumped-up feeling of a new doctor, ready for the revolution.

It is the advantage of youth, of course, to shift gears effortlessly between exhaustion and exhilaration, to come back for more after hundred-hour weeks, to take sleep deprivation like a vitamin, not a pill.

After all, this had been my dream, to be a doctor in my city, a place I was sure I knew inside and out. I gazed toward Biscayne Bay and got a flashback of growing up in Miami, of summers past, my friend Carlos's boat slicing the waves—when the engine worked, of course. We simply floated when it didn't. The bay was our pool, the beaches our playground. It was this water that kept us connected to our past, for all waters, tranquil and turbulent, seemed to flow to Miami. The place author T. D. Allman dubbed "City of the Future" in *Esquire* magazine just one year earlier invited us to wallow in her history and in it find glimpses of the millennium.

From the Caribbean pirates to the Seminole Indians, from the Everglades, that "river of grass," to Biscayne Bay, Miami's chronic state of flux became its central, most enduring theme. With each refugee migration, each summer storm, each political scandal, each building boom, the city effortlessly morphed between its multiple personalities. Cuban Casablanca. Political Pandora's box. Multiethnic laboratory. The place where *Scarface* met *Miami Vice,* just south of Disney World. The jazziest, sexiest, most sophisticated dot on the peninsula. Miami was an immigrant's city of dreams, a tourist's playground, a financier's gateway. Each identity exuded its own escapist allure, enticing refugees from the North and the South and all over the West.

How beautiful Miami seemed from the bay, the skyline and its shores so magical. Those who ventured closer undoubtedly found the tarnished underside, the expanses of poverty and suffering. The vibrant beauty of this city and the silent suffering of the poor have lived in juxtaposition since almost the beginning. The temperate zone offers all the contrasts—the wealthy and the poor, the honest and the corrupt, the glitter and the grit—all coexisting in one sprawling, teeming metropolis.

But in the eyes of a native-born intern, recently married, his first child on the way, the view outside the Jeep window was nearly breathtaking. I could trace the silver edge of a cityscape in crescendo, a newly emerging skyline of glass-and-steel structures jutting up between ornate relics from another era. I could see the tower of the nearly completed Southeast Financial Center, a fifty-five-story skyscraper that already was the tallest building south of Manhattan and east of the Mississippi River.

There it was, a crisp 1980s landscape etched by all the success stories and shining examples of the achievers and American dreamers.

And there I was, one of the dreamers, at the entrance of Jackson Memorial Hospital, JMH, one of the most prestigious medical institutions in the Southeast, a Cuban refugee boy ready for the first day of his internship. It was June 24, 1984. I now mark that as the day I entered the Miami I never knew, the one that saw the suffering and the death, the one that existed under the vaulted highways, the one you can't see from the shimmering bay, the one you can't see from your rearview mirror. ⤸

The elevator opened onto a hallway with three doors; I chose the middle one, which led to the medical intensive care unit. I should have taken it as an omen that it was the back door to the unit reserved for the most desperate cases in a public hospital.

There were eleven patients in eleven beds, all of them delicate and struggling in a setting that could have been borrowed from any public MICU in urban America. This was the place of last chances, where we gave our final and most valiant efforts to save the nearly dead. It was the gentleman in bed 9, an isolation bed, who captured my attention. I leaned forward and studied him as he lay attached to a respirator that didn't stop beeping. There he lay on his back with an endotracheal tube going down his throat and the supportive tape wrapped around his face. His wristband offered an age that seemed to belong to a man far younger than the one before me, and it gave a name he didn't respond to. Below this name and suspected date of birth, it simply read, "No Address." That meant Fire Rescue had found him on the streets of Miami. It was no wonder he looked older than his years, barely surviving on cheap wine and garbage scraps. But here is what stunned me about the patient in bed 9: he was dying of tuberculosis. Tuberculosis. It was 1984 and someone in America was dying of tuberculosis?

Bed 9 isolated not only his body but also his soul. No visitors allowed. The technology he was getting was the best in the world, the medical attention even better. It was round-the-clock science, twenty-four hours a day, seven days a week, fifty-two weeks a year, with two attending physicians, three medical residents, three medical interns, a fourth-year medical student, five nurses, five nurse assistants, and a few unit clerks—for eleven patients. So he wasn't lacking professional attention. But he was lacking human contact. I tried to communicate with him, but he didn't respond. The only clue to his past was typed on the strip of plastic around his wrist.

Where was he from?

Was he a father? I wondered.

Did he have children?

Was he a husband?

Who kept his pictures, his yearbook, his love letters?

Did he have brothers or sisters?

Did they even know he was in Miami? Did they care?

Of course they did, I assured myself.

I needed answers to these questions. Standing before this patient, I realized I was being tested on a promise I had made four years earlier, when I was a med-school student in the Dominican Republic. ⟋

I was studying on the porch on a breezy November night when I heard the telephone ring.

"Hello?" I answered.

"Chichi is dead," my mother's voice said softly.

With that phone call my world came to a halt. My little sister, my Chichi, not even eighteen years old, was gone. I felt a cold shiver emanate from inside my body, and later only numbness. She was my baby sister, the one I was supposed to protect and save. It was a duty I had embraced since I was a child, the only boy in a traditional

Cuban immigrant family. And there I was, a world away in med school, learning how to save lives, yet I could not save one so precious to me. I had failed. Even though there was absolutely no logical reason for me to have felt guilty, I did.

Chichi had been driving home from college to celebrate her eighteenth birthday and Thanksgiving when her car flipped on the highway in Palm Beach. She died instantly. Why hadn't I talked her into flying home instead of driving? Why hadn't I traveled to Gainesville to see her, instead of expecting her to meet me in Miami?

There were three other students in the car—all survived without a scratch. There on a weekday afternoon, on an unfamiliar stretch of road, she died. Our family never had a chance to say good-bye when God called for one of his favorite children.

She was beautiful, loving, and energetic. She was also humane and charitable in ways that set her apart from many of her peers. She had volunteered at the Camillus House, a homeless shelter, as a high school student, but I wouldn't know it until years after her death. I just knew God had created the sweetest soul in the world and he allowed me to be her brother. Believe it or not, we never argued.

I walked and walked that night, going no place. I knew I would miss her more than anything in the world.

My parents were devastated. My older sister was inconsolable. I began to write the eulogy and consider the meaning of her life. It was the indelible memory of her kindness and her spirit that would ultimately yield the answers to my most desperate questions, questions about the direction of my life, questions about my faith.

A few days later, I sat in the car on the way to the cemetery, helpless under the weight of my grief. I was twenty-three, and I felt old for the first time in my life. As I rode in the back of the limousine, I was numb, removed. Still, I could trace the subtle, slow-motion process of aging. It was then that I first promised my sister that if I ever became a doctor I would not let anyone die or suffer alone. For I had learned firsthand the horrible weight a family bears with any death or illness. I made a commitment to her—Chichi would not be merely a memory. She would become the loving spirit that drove my work. ⤴

Now, a man I didn't know was suffering and nobody in his world knew about it. All the science and all the attention of this great nation could not change one jarring truth: someone was dying alone. I stood at the foot of his bed, silent and powerless. I knew the greatest demons of his life, whatever tragic sequences that led to his condition, loomed far from the MICU and its morbid trappings.

Out there, in the world of a mysterious man, there was something horribly wrong. Yet all I could see were the consequences. As I walked away from the hospital that night, I decided I would set out to find his story. Outside the halls of JMH, twilight had turned the sky a steely gray. I got the feeling that my internship, and my life, was about to get intense.

Where do I start? You'd think a Miami-raised physician would know. But as I knocked on the doors of random shelters, I didn't have a clue. I asked everyone I met if they had ever seen or heard of this patient. But it was a short tour. Back in 1984, Miami's compassion for the poor wasn't one of its strong points. There were only four shelters in town—five hundred beds total. They were clustered in Downtown Miami, dim, run-down spaces on desolate, unfamiliar streets. Inside, I discovered a certain order in the constant shuffle of tattered figures, their desperation dulled by the routine. Even at this alarming extreme of poverty, there seemed to be a frightening monotony to the human stream flushing in and out of the shelters. It was as if they were part of a fringe expected to be poor, shunned as predictable, swept out of sight, at least certainly out of my sight.

I felt as if I was peering through a foreign window into a stark, deprived universe. As a med-school student, I had witnessed desperate poverty in the rural clinics of the

Dominican Republic, held starving children in my arms. But I had never seen anything like this. This was America, home of the free and, I was realizing, also of the homeless. It was the place where I had planned to finish my training before taking off to some impoverished corner of the world, someplace that really needed doctors—North Africa, Central America, the Caribbean—someplace where real desperation existed, where I could make a difference. Now I was looking through a window on that very place, just a stone's throw from the hospital.

Back at the MICU, the patient in bed 9 still didn't respond. I approached weary, overburdened social workers with his name and date of birth, but they simply shook their heads. For two weeks, I visited the neighborhood after leaving the hospital, searching the bowels of the city for a poor man's family. I stopped people on the street, asked everyone I met. No luck. Time ran out. My rotation in the MICU lasted four weeks. Unfortunately, his didn't. He died alone. I never did find his family.

Nor could I find any sense of closure in the death of this stranger. Instead of resignation, I could feel a sense of rage building inside. As I moved on to the medical wards, I realized that even in his sleep this patient had shown me something I had never seen. He guided me to a place I could never forget. Something screamed out from his silence—don't accept this death as inevitable, it said. It was my wake-up call, a strong reminder of the vow I'd made after Chichi died. No one should have to die alone, unmourned and unremembered.

In my head, scenes from the Downtown shelters played over and over, that grim window beckoning me. I searched for explanations at the medical-school library, scouring statistical data and research on homelessness. I learned only a handful of publications were willing to write about it. I learned tuberculosis was making a comeback. But nowhere did I find how this gentleman came to rest in bed 9. So I returned to that window. If I could see in, I knew there had to be a point of entry into that world. I walked the streets of Miami, searched under the overpasses, peered under the bridges to see if I could find the door.

Hanging Out

a Shingle on

Skid Row

⤙

> How can you worship a homeless man on
> Sunday and ignore one on Monday?
>> —Sign on a door at Camillus House

I T WAS A POOR MAN WHO INTRO-
duced me to the neediest of America's poor. Now it was a
wealthy man who took me a little deeper into that world.

I saw his face flash on TV one night as I was channel
surfing at home with my wife, Janus. "Look, Joe, it's Mr.
Soman."

It was my friend's father, Roger Soman, on the evening news, serving meals to the homeless. To me, Roger was always "Mr. Soman," father of Judy and Rick, one of my best buddies. He was a rich retired guy who could do anything he wanted to do in life, and there he was, doing what he wanted to do in life: feeding the poor at a place called Camillus House.

Just days earlier, I had been to Camillus looking for the family of the man who died of tuberculosis. I met the director, Brother Paul Johnson, a stand-up comic in a collar from a small Kentucky town, a man whose passion and devotion illuminated his surroundings. We clicked instantly when he told me the first dirty joke. We discovered we shared the same birthday, though he'd been cracking one-liners nineteen years longer than me. To call him charismatic is a gross understatement. He was the heart and spirit of the shelter, a man with a mission. But he never embraced the approach of the traditional soup-and-salvation shelters, where attendance at prayer services was a prerequisite for assistance. Brother Paul spared the Bible references but practiced its teachings. He was the kind of guy who truly wondered how the world could worship a homeless man on Sunday and ignore one on Monday, once posting that very message on an office door at Camillus. His jokes ranged from locker-room humor to sophisticated wit. Maybe it was the jokes that kept me coming back to Camillus, with punch lines of my own.

Soon Brother Paul had me ladling stew at the food line and sorting clothes in the storage room. He asked me to take up the usual shelter chores before he allowed me to see patients. I suspected he wanted to show me the front lines of shelter work, and then test my commitment. In time I came to learn he thought at first I was just another big-ego doctor blustering in with a lot of promises I didn't intend to keep. Now, more than fifteen years and a new clinic later, he just tells me another dirty joke. ✍

Camillus was a small, busy shelter along a decaying stretch of Northeast First Avenue, near the heart of Downtown Miami and on the edge of the district known as Overtown. The shelter, two blocks from the Freedom Tower, was opened by the Little Brothers of the Good Shepherd in 1962, to help assist the throngs of exiles escaping Fidel Castro's communist rule in Cuba. From Camillus's front door you could look up and see the coral-pink tower, our Ellis Island, the ornate edifice where Cuban refugees had been welcomed, processed, examined, and sent home with a can of government meat and a jar of generic peanut butter—not a common meal in Cuba.

Now, more than two decades later, the tower at 600

Biscayne Boulevard was a dilapidated shell of a building, a shadow of its initial grandeur. Built in 1924 during the real estate and population boom of Miami's Roaring Twenties, it was the gilded fancy of one James M. Cox, the former Ohio governor who reinvented himself as a Miami newspaper publisher after an unsuccessful run for president in 1920. The seventeen-story tower, with its splendid balconies and minarets and murals of Columbus landing in America, epitomized the era's conspicuous construction, standing as early proof that Miami's much-maligned Hispanic wealthy did not invent the term "nouveau riche."

A concrete echo of the twelfth-century Giralda Tower in Seville, Spain, it was a monument to a rich man's ego, to be pondered from his exquisite mansion across the bay. It also housed his newspaper, the *Daily News,* for thirty-two years, before being left to the whims of termites and midnight crawlers for a good five years. It would reopen in 1962 as an assistance center for half a million Cuban refugees. During its twelve-year occupation by the U.S. General Services Administration, the landmark earned its revered nickname: the Freedom Tower.

The memories of the refugees' humble beginnings in America were brought to light each time I stepped outside Camillus. I found it rather poetic that the shelter became the place where children of those early exiles would return to serve the homeless. It was 1984, and a new wave of conspicuous construction was sweeping through Downtown Miami. That was the year Miami got a new skyline.

The city was just surfacing from a spate of crises that had battered its core in the early 1980s: massive historic boatlifts from Cuba and Haiti, racial warfare in its urban heart, a murder rate that topped the national hit parade. And yet the building boom was on. The tourist and investment bucks were pouring in from South America and Europe. Multinational corporations and banks, rare entities in the Miami of the late 1970s, mushroomed across the city. The Port of Miami was jarring international statistics with its record flow of passengers and cargo. In 1984 the city picked the Rouse Company of Columbia, Maryland, to build Bayside, a $93 million shopping and entertainment complex at the old Miamarina site.

After a brief slack in foreign capital, a new boom hit the southern edge of Downtown, along Brickell Avenue. Now, three major office buildings were coming up, representing $300 million worth of construction within a space of just a few blocks. To the northwest rose Metro-Dade County's new thirty-story administrative headquarters, a $65 million hexagonal tower that would anchor Government Center.

And Downtown's crowning glory, the Southeast Financial Center, stood above it all at 764½ feet, a symbol of the futuristic city trumpeted by the politicians and the financial boosters. It was $180 million worth of polished granite and silvery glass shooting up to the stars, towering high above the desperate edges of Downtown, casting long, convenient shadows upon the inner city's festering sores, and distracting the eye upward, away from the unsightly view at ground level. Just as Cox had done sixty years earlier, the architects of this era of excess favored vertical dramatics, always aiming for the galaxy, away from the gutter.

But it was impossible to miss the shocking contrasts of life in Downtown Miami. It was most noticeable at nightfall, after the tourists left the clutter of storefronts, and the sidewalk vendors vanished, and the merchants rolled down their shutters, and the daytime office workers filed out of the skyscrapers to drive back to the burbs. In the vaporous glow of the streetlights, aimless shadows moved amid the construction rubble and trash cans. The skeletal frame of Metrorail cut across the deserted avenues. Miami's hub of enterprise transformed into an eerie Gotham City. And here, in the tense hush, the truth about Miami emerged. While the big bucks powered the construction cranes, a different kind of momentum was building on the streets. Just like the skyline, homelessness crept to new heights, fueled by the big debut of AIDS and the looming summer of crack. ⤙

*   *   *

It was a Tuesday night in the late summer of 1984 when we treated our first patients at the shelter. We set up a makeshift exam room in the sign-up office and turned the cafeteria into a waiting room. There was a desk with a clunky old computer, where the men were logged in nightly, a bureaucratic necessity to distribute equally the few beds available to the waves of homeless men in Miami. Each man down and out on his luck was allowed all the meals, clothing, and showers he needed, but only seven nights of shelter a year. It was the only fair way to make the equation work. And although the city never wanted them on the streets, the officials never offered to help them. Thank God for the Brothers of the Good Shepherd, who came to help the Cubans and stayed near the heart of America's fourth-poorest city to give it life-saving CPR.

In his mission, Brother Paul was joined by Brother René, a guy whose tall, hulking physique concealed a generous heart and gentle spirit. A soft-voiced French Canadian, René provided the perfect balance to Paul's boisterous style. It was René who would assist us on clinic nights in those early years, signing up the patients, escorting them into the exam room, fetching supplies, and later following up on that evening's medical orders. He worked quietly and briskly, injecting a sense of Zen into the greater chaos of the street clinic.

Brother René worked the front lines like nobody I had met. He loved to put people together, introduce volunteers to clients, clients to staffers, conveying the stories the homeless patients didn't feel comfortable uttering aloud, all in the spirit of improving their lives.

It was Brother René who took me into the kitchen one afternoon to meet Jim. He was a member of our crew, the team of homeless men who had used up their yearly allotment of seven nights at the shelter but had earned the right to live and work at Camillus because they had shown an extraordinary commitment to getting off the streets and off the drugs. That day, Jim was cleaning the kitchen after having served lunch to about twelve hundred other homeless individuals. We found him scrubbing pots, his linebacker torso hunched over the sink. He was a tall, prematurely balding guy, in his late twenties, undoubtedly a former jock, I surmised.

As I prepared to greet Jim with a handshake, I thought of what Brother René had told me about him moments earlier: "We have to help Jim get out of his shell. Why don't you go out and play basketball with him? I think it'll really help his self-confidence."

Jim's hello was a quick, polite nudge of his elbow— his hands were full of soap. His eyes never met mine. His words were clipped and barely audible.

"So I hear you're a jock," I ventured. "Wanna go shoot hoops sometime?"

He looked up and nodded.

"Yeah, sure," he mumbled.

Jim eventually became one of our first volunteers at the clinic, helping Brother René with intake. His shyness and reserved manner hid the tumult of his past, as well as his deep intellect and knowledge. He knew several languages—English, Spanish, French, and Creole—but he chose not to speak any of them very much. With the patients, though, he showed warmth and compassion, important traits for our rudimentary medical setup.

We kept it simple: just sign up and we'll take care of you. Of my first ten patients, eight had foot problems, severe infections from ill-fitting shoes or from barefoot treks through rat-infested, trash-strewn underpasses. So, I thought after the eighth set of diseased soles, this is what I went to med school for, to be an improvised podiatrist? Hell, I wanted to be a liver doctor—but I was in for a detour first.

I remember a patient who came in one night in early July 1984 complaining of foot pain. He was a young laborer, sun-blistered and still clothed in the musty shirt of that day's work. When he pulled off one shoe and sock, his foot gave off a stinging odor that gave away the diagnosis: a severe fungal infection.

Actually, his was a relatively simple medical problem.

The treatment required to heal it, however, was a more complicated story.

"My feet burn like hell, Doc," he told me.

Damn, I thought as I helped him remove his other shoe, *another foot problem.* I had already seen my share of such cases. I could recognize that pungency of infection from across the room. I got accustomed to practicing my old med-school technique of breathing through the mouth.

"Well, it looks like we have a bad case of athlete's foot," I said. "Pretty common down here this time of the year, with the humidity and the rain."

It was summer and the seasonal thunderstorms had hit hard, the way they had for as long as I could remember. As a kid, I would try to outrace the sudden afternoon downpours, barely staying ahead of the slanting sheets of rain on my scramble toward home. Sometimes I would arrive drenched and shivering, happy to slip under cover and into dry clothes.

That evening at the clinic, my patient had neither cover nor dry clothes. Therefore, even the most simple remedy rang ridiculous. I started to say, "All you have to do is wear clean and dry socks every day . . . ," but then I caught myself and tried again:

"Well, if that's not possible, try to wash and dry your feet every night when you come back from work. And sleep barefoot to avoid the extra humidity."

"I work the labor pool, Doc. I live under a bridge. It rains all the time. The rats come out at night. I gotta keep my feet covered. I don't want my toes bitten off."

Indeed, I had a true dilemma. What disease should I let my patient suffer from—severe infection, or the consequences of rat bites? This man would benefit from a strong antifungal cream, a costly remedy and one I couldn't offer at the clinic that night.

"I'll meet you here tomorrow night, seven o'clock, with some socks and some medication, okay?" I offered.

The following evening, the patient returned. I gave him a six-pack of white socks and a tube of antifungal cream, courtesy of the pharmaceutical stash at JMH. I like to think the remedy worked, since I never saw him again. But his condition taught me something I would always remember at the clinic and under the bridges: that every medical treatment, even the simplest ones, must be tailored to suit individuals, not just diseases. It is a lesson I have taken to medical students, one I've made a central theme of my lectures on treating the homeless. No textbook will teach you how to gauge all the factors of the street into a diagnosis or a treatment. Only your patients can do that. Sometimes the solutions to the most complex medical dilemmas are contained in the stories of their lives. And sometimes you have to be more of a jazz musician than a doctor, allowing yourself to improvise on a standard. ✐

*   *   *

The awkward exchange with the foot patient taught me there was so much I still didn't know about treating the homeless. For that matter, I didn't know anything about public health, turf wars, or the politics of poverty. I was young and stupid (of course, I didn't know that yet, either).

At least I was smart enough, however, to know what I *didn't* know. If I was to follow my heart and help those in need, then I required more information. I went to see Alina Perez-Stable, the social worker on our clinic floor at Jackson Memorial Hospital and the daughter of one of my mentors, Dr. Eliseo Perez-Stable.

I found her in her office, tucked in the back of the third floor.

"So, what do you know about the homeless?" I blurted out, stepping through her office door.

Alina looked up from her work and gave me a puzzled look. "Excuse me—good afternoon, Joe. What about the homeless?"

I began to tell her about my experiences at Camillus, about the horrible cases I had seen.

"You gotta see this, Alina. You won't believe this is happening in our own backyard," I pressed. I saw her eyes light up with a glint of outrage. I realized I was preaching to the choir. Alina was a disciplined professional, but she had inherited her father's humanitarian soul.

Suddenly she snapped back in her chair, as if she had remembered something important.

"Wait a minute! I met this guy from Portland at a conference. He's the guy we have to call," she said, reaching for her Rolodex.

We? Inside I beamed at her effortless camaraderie. It was always like that with Alina and me. We clicked on the important things in health care. We didn't have to explain the world to each other. We didn't have to dissect ethical grays. If it was right, it was right. She got it.

She pulled out a card printed with the number for a VA hospital in Oregon.

"This is the guy," she said, handing me the card. "Dr. James Reuler. Call him."

Dr. Reuler, as it turned out, was a nationally acclaimed Portland physician who had started the Wallace Medical Concern, a free walk-in clinic staffed by students. I was a putzy intern with a foreign degree. But he returned my call one night while I was on rotation in the MICU. From a hallway telephone, I nervously introduced myself and asked him to tell me about his clinic. We talked about everything from the most commonly used medications to the diseases most frequently treated. I was charged up. I hung up the phone high on hope, ready to save the free world. I found his work so inspiring that I decided to base the name of our clinic on his—the word "concern" said it all. I had no formal training in public health, no equipment, no medication or supplies, no malpractice coverage. But I had a valuable recruit—Alina, another child of Cuban refugees—and I had a name: the clinic on Miami's skid row would become the Camillus Health Concern. ✐

I didn't have a clue about operational requirements, budgets, and inventories. I was blinded by big Schweitzeresque dreams of a revolution. Why shouldn't it be revolutionary, this clinic? The drastic scenario I was witnessing at Camillus screamed for drastic measures. I knew it was an echo of a national epidemic, a direct result of America's attitudes toward the poor. But I also knew free clinics were few and far between. And I knew it would take more than the clinic itself to make a dent in the cycle. It would take a valiant army of medical students, and an academic curriculum to reinforce the battalions.

These were big dreams, but they led to even bigger realities. We couldn't even imagine it then, but when I became the first assistant dean of homeless education at the University of Miami School of Medicine in 1991, we would be the first school in the nation to establish a course on homelessness, the first to run rotations of med students through homeless clinics, feature lectures on homelessness, and explore health care alternatives for the poor. My early students were the foot soldiers who helped inspire the school's commitment.

We labored Tuesday and Thursday nights for four years, seeing anyone who walked in and signed up, our efforts underwritten by blood and guts and whatever supplies we could stuff into our briefcases at the hospital. I guess we had a bit of a Robin Hood mentality. We didn't need money, just our *ganas*, our *cojones*, a belief we were doing God's work—and, of course, a five-finger discount on supplies.

It would take us those four years to realize we needed to raise money. In the meantime, we discovered a wealth of goodwill and services in kind. Where did all the generosity come from? I confess I didn't stop to ask what was prompting the enthusiasm. I can only speak for my own drive. I was overwhelmed with a sense of mission and purpose—not to mention that I found the work tremendously exciting, with its unexpected nightly twists. I was fired up. At times I felt like a relentless salesman, out there recruiting. Never once did I expect to have a door slammed in my face. While I found a tremendous degree of ignorance concerning the poor and homeless, I also found great compassion each time I stopped to describe the world I had stumbled upon. I realized that even the educated needed to be educated.

The eagerness to help contrasted starkly with the political backdrop of the day. It was the Reagan eighties, a period of widening economic chasms and ruthless cutbacks of social programs. Still, it was easy to recruit social-minded doctors and nurses, volunteers to step up to the plate. We had a goal: hassle-free medicine. No insurance forms. No bureaucracy. No managed-care second-guessing. No issue of economics. No cover-your-ass documentation, only the basics: "White male. Twenty-eight. Infected foot, left. Fungal."

The social workers would take it from there, exploring the wasteland that was Florida's social-support services for basic follow-up assistance. In my eyes, these were the true miracle workers, those who found beds that didn't exist, spaces in rare and overbooked recovery programs.

For all the headaches, the chaos was attractive—and contagious. Whenever I talked about the homeless to my fellow interns, I found ready volunteers in every significant way. Good friends offered to donate equipment, medications, time. Our first volunteers included a doctor named Mark O'Connell and a pair of physician brothers named Harrington, Bill and Tom. Together we explored the gritty world under the highways, visiting patients and spreading the word about our clinic. An O'Connell, two

Harringtons, and a Greer—we called ourselves the IBT, the Irish Bridge Team, even though we spent a lot of time speaking Spanish.

Then it was time to teach what my father, also a physician and perhaps my greatest teacher, had taught me: the compassion of medicine. The clinic became a hub for University of Miami med students, all fresh-faced, enthusiastic, and ready to save the world, stethoscopes dangling off their necks. They called themselves Camillus Heads. They were the top students, in both academics and desire. It was encouraging to see them at work. They got it. They had no designs on some obscure corner of the Third World. With all their youth, they were mature enough to grasp the realities and needs of their own city. They saw that their responsibility as doctors was to take care of people, without judgment or prejudice. They became so tightly knit that even their group identity evolved. They actually came to me one day, the guys with their long hair and earrings, the girls with their tie-dyed, retrochic dresses, and said, "We're going to change our name. Camillus Heads is too sixties, man."

So from then on they became known as PW-GAS, which stood for People Who Give A Shit.

The students, who really gave a shit about matters of social policy, sponsored two educational forums at the med-school campus. They wanted to know, during a time of presidential elections, why the real issues they faced each day were being ignored by the media. They invited a top ABC News producer and the publisher of the *Miami Herald* to answer their questions. The posters went up all over campus: "People Who Give A Shit sponsor Paul Mason, producer, ABC News, and Dave Lawrence Jr., publisher of the *Miami Herald*."

In small letters at the bottom, the posters said: "Faculty adviser: Pedro J. Greer Jr., M.D."

The forum was a roaring success with the students. The house was packed, the questions exhausting, the debate energetic. But it just so happened that the university's board of trustees had chosen that same day to have their monthly meeting on the medical-school campus. A couple of days later, I was called into the dean's office. He asked me about this club of ours. A trustee, he said, had pointed out the curious name.

Yes, I offered, I approved the name. It was a good name—it put the spirit of the club in a nutshell, I argued. Well, said the dean, who was actually our greatest supporter at the university, can't we compromise and just use the initials?

So we agreed. The new club would be simply PW-GAS, or People Who Give A S———.

I didn't complain. It happens.

*   *   *

Tuesday and Thursday nights were always jam-packed at Camillus. Each patient added a stroke of color to the grim urban landscape unfolding before me; each reinforced the toughest rule of being a doctor: that we are allowed to judge only the illness, never the person.

I remember one of the first patients I saw. He walked in looking like hell warmed over and smelling like cheap rum. Unshaven, disheveled, a sling around his right arm, he shuffled in, never looking up, as if he didn't have the strength to lift his head. At first glance I could see only the sadness of his present state, no trace of his luminous past. He needed a shower, some rest, a clean sling, and forty-eight to seventy-two hours of detox under observation to make sure he didn't go into severe DTs (delirium tremens) or seizures. The public detox center, which was always helpful to us, had no beds that night. As we did in such cases, we provided a bed and enough space for his meager possessions so that we could observe him ourselves that night. As soon as he settled in, he revealed a remarkable story. Displayed on the wall beside his bunk was a diploma from Notre Dame. There, too, was a framed photograph of a fighter jet. It was the one he flew over Korea during the war. The room was smaller than my college dorm room, but it held one American's proud story. Over the years he pulled himself together and did well, eventually moving to Costa Rica, where he had friends. I heard from him a couple of years ago. He sounded good. He was dry. I hung up that phone filled with hope. This is what we were supposed to be doing.

In the end, like so many patients living at the bottom rung of poverty, all he needed was time and compassion. There he was, a U.S. war veteran whose poverty and personal demons had derailed his life. But in the eyes of the country he served, he was a no-name bum. America looks upon its poorest citizens as failures, screwups. That's why its health care system is designed for an upper-middle-class society, why the poor and uninsured are left to scramble on the fringes. It is a system of cookie-cutter remedies that imposes unrealistic expectations upon the poor, that dispenses prescriptions that simply don't translate under a bridge. It expects a homeless diabetic to eat three balanced meals a day and dutifully inject the prescribed dose of insulin, get plenty of rest and fluids—and don't forget that midnight snack. Nowhere in the script is the part where the heroin junkie rips off your needle, where that day's trash offers only fried-chicken bones, where the rats keep you awake at night. Nowhere. ⌐

So it went every Tuesday and Thursday night—seeing patients, mostly men, and trying to heal the wounds on their bodies and the aches in their souls with only our hands and whatever we brought with us that night. In America it seemed as if we didn't care if you suffered, but if you were about to die we'd scramble to save you at JMH—and then send you back to suffer, to the streets.

So I can't say I felt too guilty about slipping supplies out of the ER at Jackson, stashing in my briefcase gauze and tape and samples to take back to the patients at Camillus. After all, weren't these the same patients I might eventually take care of in the ER, anyway? That's how I justified it. And then I said two Hail Marys and an Our Father.

The big stash, however, came in 1987 with the remodeling of the Miami VA hospital, which had cleaned out tons of old office and medical equipment. Lucky for us, their chief of medicine was a generous man: Dr. Perez-Stable. Leave it to Alina's dad to figure a way out of the supply-room bureaucracy. In no time I was standing in a warehouse in Hialeah, surrounded by examination tables, chairs, desks, surgical equipment, all the tools to build a dream clinic. I made arrangements to return and pick up what we needed.

I borrowed my father's pickup truck and drove to Camillus to look for a moving crew. One of the first volunteers was a squat, muscular, tough-as-nails Nuyorican guy, freshly released from prison up north. Riding shotgun, he turned out to be a chatty, outgoing guy. A ponytail dangled down his back and tattoos covered his arms and neck, street-issued passport stamps for seedy destinations in the underbelly of New York and its prisons. Well into our drive to Hialeah, I found out why he had been in jail: he killed a guy by punching him in the neck during a street fight. So, great, there I was in the time of *Miami Vice,* a Cuban doctor in a truck with a convicted murderer, on my way to a warehouse to pick up a load of government-owned equipment for free. Once inside, I got a kid-in-a-candy-store rush looking at all the goodies. We came away with a set of green VA waiting chairs, exam tables, desks, everything. We even took a stainless-steel whirlpool—what for, I still haven't a clue. It would sit there, unused, for years, a reminder of our ragtag beginnings and big dreams.

Now that we had furnished the inside, it was time to build the outside—of a new clinic. Camillus had existed for about two years in its original storefront location. We were bursting at the seams from day one, and eventually we'd expanded into some connecting office space when it became available. Now it was time for an even bigger expansion. Brother Paul had acquired an adjacent lighting store through some convoluted ninety-nine-year lease that was a mystery to all of us except him. That was the thing about Brother Paul—he had this knack for getting something for almost nothing, a wonderful gift that comes in handy when you're trying to provide services for the poor.

With our new (to us, anyway) clinic equipment waiting in the wings, we were ready to hire a contractor, and I knew just the man for the job—Carlos Santeiro, a friend since our families' arrival in America. In our carefree high school days, we'd navigate the bay in his little boat and admire the cityscape. Now Carlos was a big-time contractor who had done his part to enhance that view with gleaming buildings and elaborate works. I was hoping he'd do the same for skid row. When he heard my proposal, he wanted to help.

"Look, Carlos," I told him, "you've got to come in with the lowest bid." The fact was, there were no other bidders, but since he didn't ask, I didn't tell him. I bombarded him with pleading phone calls. I even faxed him pictures of homeless children. He was amused at my needless lobbying—of course he'd do it, he said. And he did, constructing our first clinic under cost and ahead of schedule.

The only trouble was, the city would not give us a certificate of occupancy unless we rebuilt the sidewalks, at a cost of $8,000. For that amount, we could treat twice the number of patients we were seeing at that time. We were outraged. This was the city that didn't give a damn if the homeless had beds. But they were insisting on spiffy sidewalks? This was the city that herded busloads of Nicaraguan refugees into its old baseball stadium, Bobby Maduro, but then refused to let the homeless use the same facility because it wasn't "up to code." This was the city that advocates would eventually sue for its dehumanizing treatment of the homeless. We chose to ignore the demand. Let them try to close us down, we dared them. To this day, there is no occupational license for that space.

If I had to describe it, I'd say our decor was a mix of vintage voluntary donation and early reluctant philanthropy. I remember one of my private patients, a wealthy, rather grumpy older man who wore his gruff demeanor like an Armani suit. He was the kind of guy who would donate generously in a blink for scientific research. But he wanted nothing to do with the homeless. They were screwups, in his book. Still, he showed up at the medical grand-round lecture I gave on homelessness, a talk I called "The Medical Consequences of Inappropriate Social Policies."

That night he called me with these words: "Look, I don't care about the homeless. It just really bothers me when they're sick."

That turned out to be an odd disclaimer for a big donation: he gave us $150,000 for the clinic. When I invited him down to see the clinic, he looked around and declared it a "shit hole." He was right. That earned us another donation—cabinetry and a new carpet. The carpet lent a cushy feel to an otherwise grim scene. He gave us more than money and furniture. He taught us that aesthetics had a lot to do with respect for our fellow human beings.

We tried to keep the rug spotless, but it was next to impossible. Not long after the carpet was installed, we had a bloody emergency. A homeless man staggered in with a profusely bleeding stab wound in the base of his neck. He was holding a wadded-up T-shirt to the cut, just under his clavicle, but he couldn't stop the bleeding—the downward stab had hit a vein.

"No! No! Bring him in the back, quick!" We ran out to the waiting area and brought the patient into the back, trying to stop the bleeding and spare the carpet from the blood gushing out of his wound. Of course, we learned it was next to impossible to keep a rug perfect when the most violent streets of Miami sometimes detoured through our front door.

Though we were helping a population in need, nevertheless it seemed futile to wage a revolution from inside a clinic. Somehow we had to meet the disasters before they stumbled into Camillus. I needed to go deeper under the bridges.

Under

the Bridge

⤎

The place is a war zone—gutted, bombed out.

—*Tropic* magazine

WHERE WAS THIS FLOW OF HOMEless patients coming from? Where was its hellish source? Those who came to the clinic described dwellings too desperate to believe. And these were the patients who had made it to our door. What about the others? How many even knew our clinic existed? How many simply languished?

I set out to spread the word in my Jeep, navigating the underpasses, pulling up within walking distance of what turned out to be some of the worst living conditions I've seen anywhere. My intention was not to treat these would-be patients amid their squalor, but simply to let them know we existed, to invite them to come down to the clinic. In the most urgent of instances, we'd carry out the sick and transport them to Camillus. But mostly, we pounded the weeded pavement, spreading the gospel of free health care for the indigent.

In my treks, I discovered that the eastern stretch of I-395 concealed a tunnel of despair. The highway arched toward Biscayne Bay, carrying tourists, revelers, and Miami's children of the sun to popular beaches, trendy nightclubs, and the outdoor cafés of Ocean Drive. On its way to the land of recess and excess, it passed the gleaming cruise ships, the millionaire mansions of Star Island, and even a seaplane terminal. But beneath this highway, just around North Miami Avenue, there existed a decaying, makeshift village. To the homeless who lived there, it came to be known as the Dungeon. Later, the press would dub this place the Mudflats.

Its north side had a wall, a decline onto a puddle-filled dirt floor. Just yards from the brassy flow of Biscayne Boulevard, the people of the Mudflats hung sheets of chain-link fence between concrete pillars, padded them with musty bedding, tattered rugs, and pieces of foam rubber. There, in nests of garbage, they lived.

The first time I climbed this embankment, I felt as if I was not climbing at all, but rather descending into another realm. People peered out of cardboard boxes. Putrid smoke from the crack pipes formed clouds in the stagnant, humid afternoon. I remember the listless gaze of a man who sat with a needle stuck, dangling, in his leg.

The Mudflats would become a symbol of the city's spreading homeless crisis, a portrait of undeniable despair that put Miami on the map of an alarming national trend. The plight of the homeless was thrust onto a national plane in the mid-1980s, about the time a homeless man froze to death in a telephone booth in Washington, D.C. In 1984, when we were getting our clinic off the ground, an advocate named Mitch Snyder staged a fifty-one-day hunger strike, forcing President Reagan to turn an abandoned federal building into a homeless shelter. But D.C. was just one of many cities affected by the newly visible homeless epidemic, which stretched from San Francisco to New York, from Los Angeles to Miami.

In Downtown Miami, the area under I-395, the Mudflats, would become the familiar backdrop for TV news stories and a pilgrimage stop for advocates of social change. I guess it was here, in the land of the invisible, that I became visible. Lured by the compelling scenes, reporters and news crews shadowed me, requested unofficial tours and quotable sound bites. I welcomed my fifteen minutes of fame, hoping to raise awareness and empathy in jaded Miami, where drivers routinely shooed away street-corner window washers.

I sometimes took my own camera on these treks through the Mudflats, to document what my eyes couldn't believe: ramshackle homes made of cardboard boxes, crack dens billowing pink smoke across stagnant mud puddles, cavelike dwellings promising cocaine extremes and equalizing devastation. The people inside these lean-tos often seemed like zombies, belonging to another dimension. I'd weave around the boxes and the trash to find those who would be my patients. I would photograph only those who gave me permission to do so. Later, I would show these pictures during lectures to students, hoping to rev them into the same state of urgency I felt when I snapped them.

It was in these Mudflats that Florida's Governor Lawton Chiles, facing the critical peak of homelessless, would declare a state of emergency, setting in motion a hands-on response from Miami's civic and corporate leaders.

And it was in the Mudflats, in 1989, that I met a very sick gentleman named Jean Philippe. I found him on a day when a *Miami Herald* reporter followed me under the bridge on my rounds. Some patients at the clinic had told me about Jean Philippe, a man in the Mudflats too feeble to walk. We had crossed an obstacle course of broken glass and ankle-deep gravel and ash.

"The place is a war zone—gutted, bombed out. There is nothing but trash for the eye to focus on," the reporter, Meg Laughlin, would later write in her Sunday magazine story.

"Don't get too close. I smell," Jean Philippe said in a near whisper.

He was emaciated, lying on a discarded, filthy old foam-rubber pad at the top of the embankment, just underneath the overpass. Just yards away, farther down the sloping patch of ground, the fires from cocaine pipes crackled brightly. I put my hand on his aching belly. I could feel a swell of the disease and his body contracting, defending against the pressure of my hand. The pain, he told me, had grown more severe in recent months. He had been to the emergency room at Jackson Memorial Hospital twice, only to be dismissed as a simple gastritis patient and discharged hours later. He was sent home with the wrong diagnosis and a standard prescription for a man with a substandard life: take Tagamet at night, eat a soft diet, get plenty of rest. (Right. That and a two-week Caribbean vacation to escape the stresses of city life?) It turns out Jean Philippe had a hole in his stomach from a giant ulcer, but by the time the attending physician made the correct diagnosis, the patient had disappeared back to the Dungeon.

His illness was a metaphor for his very existence in the diaspora.

"Where are you from?" I asked him.

Staring across the firelit crack den, Jean Philippe cleared his throat. "Cité Soleil," he replied in a raspy voice, naming the poorest shantytown in the Haitian capital. As he spoke, his story echoed the heartache of so many refugee sagas: he had arrived in the United States with so many dreams, sailing to Florida on a boat three years earlier.

"So, how does this compare to Haiti?" I asked him, in a futile attempt to make small talk.

Jean Philippe paused. Cars roared overhead. Even though it was early in the afternoon, it seemed very dark.

"This," he said at last, "is worse than Cité Soleil."

My God, I thought, did this corner of Miami rank below the worst of slums in the poorest country of the Western Hemisphere?

Jean Philippe didn't smoke crack, but he was so frail he was forced to rely on the charity of the addicts who surrounded him. And even when they could find nothing else to eat, someone always brought him milk. That day, I pulled a couple of dollars from my pocket and handed them to a bystander, hoping he, too, would come back with milk for Jean Philippe. Then I told my new patient to stay calm and rest. I promised I would return and take him to the clinic. He nodded.

As I looked behind me, to the south, I could see a ten-foot-high fence with gaps in its chain link, the entrance to this miserable village. I meandered through the random arrangement of human nests, introducing myself to the residents.

"What's up? I'm Dr. Joe from the clinic at Camillus," I'd volunteer. "Come by and visit."

The boom of my hellos echoed strangely in the caverns of the Mudflats as I walked south. I could see the small building where homeless men gathered in the morning to sell their labor to pickup trucks for slave wages. Getting hired carried the prize of a fifteen-hour day in the hot sun, in 95 percent humidity, all for about fifteen bucks.

Many of these workers dwelled in a large open field of overgrown lots known as No Man's Land. Eventually, the Miami Arena, home of the newly minted Miami Heat, would be built on that site. The gleaming pink Miami Arena cost $50 million to construct in 1988, lavish digs for a team with a rocky start. This pre–Pat Riley ensemble would go on to lose its first seventeen games. But Miami politicians held the team up as part of a promise to clean up blighted Overtown, as the district was officially called. Of course, "clean up," in politician lingo, meant cosmetic strokes, which meant homeless sweeps. Miami city commissioners would debate whether or not to arrest the homeless on the nights of Heat games. I would suggest to them that in view of the team's record and the arena's cost to taxpayers, they should consider arresting the coach instead. Of course, it would never come to a vote, so there would be no official policy. They would just keep harrassing and arresting people who lived on the street. ⤳

Hardly anything that was built in Overtown was ever built for Overtown. And there is little wonder why the area grew into one of Miami's most blighted neighborhoods.

I knew it hadn't always been like this. In the days of segregation, Overtown was a thriving African-American enclave bustling with small businesses, nightlife, and a vibrant community. Designed by racist laws and Jim Crow, this district across the railroad tracks, just to the west of white Downtown, became a hub for U.S. and Caribbean blacks, professionals and workers alike. It was a district marked by a strong sense of community, a haven for visiting black entertainers forced by Miami Beach's white establishment to lodge in "separate but equal" quarters clear "over town." So it wasn't unusual for a visitor to find late-night jam sessions, featuring stars like Josephine Baker, at any of the small hotels or clubs that lined the district called Little Broadway.

But in the mid-1950s, the neighborhood's death was foretold by the cement pillars punctuating the streets. As the foundation was set for the steely gray bridges of the interstate highway, residents were forced to sell or vacate their properties. Those whose homes were not literally displaced by I-95 and its auxiliary highways rightfully feared land value would plummet. Overtown would never be the same. A steel dagger had been driven through its heart, in the name of progress.

How ironic it is that Overtown's most desperate residents one day would end up wandering the vast expanses under those very vaulted highways, the wasted land in the bosom of town. The expressway and its squalid underside embodied both the cause and the consequence of neglect.

Overtown itself became a metaphor for how America's invisible get screwed over, repeatedly betrayed. ↱

That particular day, the invisible man's name was Jean Philippe. We returned to transport him to the clinic the next day. His move from the Dungeon to shelter proved symbolic, a shift from darkness to light. At the shelter, this patient maintained a great disposition, even though his pain didn't go away with the standard medications. I took him to JMH for an endoscopic procedure. I checked his esophagus, stomach, duodenum, and small bowel for lesions. I found what was one of the largest ulcers I had ever seen. Luckily, we were able to sign him up for an experimental drug to treat ulcers.

Jean Philippe turned out to be the most compliant patient in the protocol, even though he lived in a shelter, without transportation or family nearby. The medicine worked and his stomach no longer hurt. He took on a job at Camillus, where he still works helping other homeless men.

I guess this is where the strings should swell, at the crest of a happy ending. But in the desolate gravity field connecting Camillus to the Mudflats, the sound track was predictably ominous. After months of probing the depths of it, the sounds, the sights, and the smells were becoming familiar to me.

One Saturday morning, I was driving by the Miami River and spotted a small group of homeless men. I parked my Jeep and walked toward the river to say hello. Just months earlier, theirs was a world entirely foreign to me. But that day, for the first time, they said hello because they recognized me. I think they were actually glad to see me. I realized that not only had I entered the other side, I had become part of its tenuous landscape. That's not to say I was growing immune to the periodic shocks of the street.

The Night

Elvis Died

⌁

Yeah, here comes Dr. Rambo.
—Overtown resident

Yeah, there goes Mother Teresa.
—Overheard at
Jackson Memorial Hospital

Aw, come on, you're gonna let some Cuban boy kick your ass in hoops?" I teased Jim as he pounded across the weed-choked court. We were playing one-on-one on a shabby rectangle of asphalt in the middle of Overtown. It had become a male-bonding ritual for us, although more than once the rivalry proved uneven—it was usually me who would get my ass whooped.

Just then, as he put in a three-pointer, he gave me a sly smile, walked to the foul line, and said: "Naw. Don't think so."

I could measure the depth of our growing friendship in his increasing on-court jabs, his old shy self shed during our game. It was a far cry from the first time we went out to the courts, at the edge of a small park. We walked past the drug holes and punched-out facades, took a shortcut through a hole in the fence of one apartment building. I walked ahead of Jim with the ball under my arm, pumped for the game. Then I realized the footsteps behind me had stopped. I turned to find only my shadow. Jim was nowhere in sight. Feeling conspicuous and alone in unfamiliar grounds, I headed for the exit, trying to appear casual and just part of the neighborhood. I searched for Jim around the block, my bewilderment growing as I debated whether or not call out his name. At last, I found him waiting for me around the other side of the apartment complex.

"Where the hell'd you go?" I demanded.

"Well, Joe," he replied with a laugh, "you're the only white guy around. Everyone's gonna think you look like a cop. What am I supposed to do?"

I realized that had been my initiation, a test of sorts. Jim wanted to see if I had the intestinal fortitude to hang around. I had passed because I didn't freak out. From that day on, we were famous buddies. Jim was a quick-footed ballplayer with a hell of an outside shot. He shuffled around me as the sun cast long shadows across the asphalt. In them lay the painful secrets of his past. He was from the Midwest, smart as hell, educated at a Catholic orphanage when his mother abandoned him. He went to college on a football scholarship and thrived. With less than a year to go before graduation, his life turned again. Out of nowhere, his mother reappeared. I never asked him what happened—and he never offered to tell me—but I know his mother's presence sent his life into a tailspin. He dropped out of college and headed for Miami in a drug haze, eventually landing at Camillus.

Somehow, it was this stranger to Overtown who made me feel I could fit in the 'hood. ⤙

At first, I'd slip in as a civilian. But I began to realize my intended patients were confusing me for a cop, as Jim had suggested. Not that I blame them—there I was, an ex–football player with a taste for doughnuts, sporting a black leather jacket and a mustache. Then, one day during my rounds under the bridges, I turned to find a Saturday night special pointed at my head. I threw my arms up and managed an introduction.

"I'm Dr. Joe Greer," I said, realizing that probably meant squat to a crack addict with a gun.

He looked at me defiantly, still pointing the barrel between my eyes, and scoffed.

"No you ain't. Dr. Greer is fat."

"Well," I replied, rather amused, "whatever drug you're on, it has some advantages."

Trying to buy time for his cocaine frenzy to wear off, I made idle conversation. But none of my usual lines seemed to be working. Finally, when the smoke cleared from his brain, his eyes once again focused on my true proportions.

"Sorry, Doc," he said, stepping back and shaking his head. "You should wear a lab coat or something."

That's when I started wearing a lab coat.

The initiation rites of the underpasses could be daunting. Getting street-toughened guys to trust you, particularly when you were bouncing around their turf in a white coat, required heavy doses of sheer gall—and zero doses of ego. You had to be ready to take the jabs from the peanut gallery, the nicknames and catcalls.

"Yeah, here comes Dr. Rambo," went one familiar cry. I took it in stride. Besides, I was used to worse jabs back at the hospital, in the doctors' dining quarters. "Yeah, there goes Mother Teresa," went one familiar hiss.

So I figured my place as a doctor in the streets would be secure as long as I kept showing up, taking the stares and the jabs, proving that I wasn't going to be run off by a few bullies. And the amazing thing is, not only did the homeless accept me as one of the brotherhood, they also defended me as a comrade in arms. They guarded my car. They kept the bad guys away. They put the word out— touch the Doc and you're history. It all became clear one day when I was at the clinic. I had been on call the night before, and I was beat. Absentmindedly, I had left my overnight call bag and my good camera in the car, which was parked right in front of the clinic.

While I was inside seeing patients, someone broke into my car and stole the bag, the camera, and the expensive lens. Oh, this is great, I thought. I can afford this. I have a wife back home, pregnant with our second child. I'm making almost no money at the hospital—like $15,000 a year. I've been up all night. And some idiot breaks into my car, shatters my window, and steals all my stuff.

I felt a rush of my tough-boy *cubanito* inner child. This loser might as well have been the school-yard bully back in old Westchester, the Miami neighborhood I grew up in. I darted out of the clinic and headed for Overtown. Not until later did I realize what I must have looked like:

there I was with my black leather jacket and an attitude. I *did* look like a cop.

A few of my homeless patients had tracked the guy down, but he'd already sold my camera for crack. He actually had the *cojones* to try to sell me back the rest of my things.

"Just gimme back my stuff," I demanded.

But the guy, a coked-up hood with tattoos all over his body, had other ideas. He took a swing at my face. So I hit him back—and grabbed for my stuff. My homeless accomplices handed me all the other possessions he had taken—from other victims. As I said, "No, thank you," and shook their hands, I felt a sharp pain from their grip. Then I noticed a swelling in my right hand. I had broken my right ring finger with the punch. The hood went to jail for grand theft—with a busted nose. And I headed back to the clinic with a fractured finger.

When I got back to my car, I found all the shattered glass neatly swept up, all the loose change in my car stacked in tidy piles on the dash. Some patients from the clinic, homeless men, had done this for me. People who you might expect to steal from you were the ones apologizing that it happened at all. I was protected by some strange sort of brotherhood. I realized I was more than a doctor to them. They had my back. They had the clinic's back.

I realized time buys respect. Of course, a street fight

in the inner city speeds up the process—especially if you're fighting the bad guy.

After that, I knew the clinic would be safe. We had no problem seeing patients late into the evenings, though across the street from the clinic sat a burned-out building, a crack den.

One night at about ten o'clock, having seen one crack-related problem after another, from addicts with chest pains to addicts with paranoia, all coming from the drug hole across the way, I was ready to call it a night. I had worked at the hospital all day, hadn't seen my family since the night before. But they kept lighting up, freaking out, and rushing across the street to the clinic. It was time to close the bar. My Cuban-Irish temper flared up again. I darted across the street, dodging an eighteen-wheeler in the crossing, and headed into the crack house, where I made this announcement: "Will ya please quit smoking that shit so I can go home?"

Then I stormed out as quickly as I had stormed in. To them, in the context of a crack-induced paranoia, I must have been like a cop staging a drug bust (even though I wasn't wearing my leather jacket).

Years later, a man approached me outside the clinic and extended his hand in a greeting. He looked as though he might be a community volunteer or a potential donor, well dressed and articulate. But he wasn't.

"I just came by to say thank you," he began.

"For what?" I asked.

"I don't know if you remember, but one night years ago, you walked into a building, over there," he said, signaling toward the razed lot where the old crack house once stood. "I was there that night you came in and told us to stop smoking. Scared the hell out of everybody. You scared me straight. I just wanted to tell you. Thanks."

Unfortunately, my outburst didn't have the same effect on everyone around. One case in point: a kid named Ice. I never learned his real name, but he was a slightly built, baby-faced kid, the son of a Southern preacher, a streetwise hustler who loved to joke that only Brother Paul could outhustle him. Ice was a regular at the shelter and at the clinic, but he was also a fixture in the neighborhood crack dens. Through the years, the scars of street living had transformed his face, his smile broken by a gash that ran from the edge of his mouth across his cheek. But his hustling techniques never changed.

"Hey, Doc, take care of the car for you? Clean the car for you? Got any money for me?" went his routine.

I'd always give him one of my stock answers: "You sound like one of my kids."

"Come on, Doc, you know me."

"And you know me, Ice. You think I'm gonna carry money in this neighborhood?"

It was always the same. He remains on the street, ubiquitous, unreachable. ⟿

The years passed as we trained at the hospital and spent our "spare" time trying to help the homeless. We had built a free clinic, the only clinic in Overtown and the only free clinic in Miami, and had fanned out under the bridges to spread the word to a population of reluctant patients. As I drove throughout the bowels of Miami looking for anyone who needed a doctor, I learned that the west side of North Miami Avenue was just like the east side in its dark, mean, and dusty conditions, except it was meaner and dustier. This is where I would return with the Tuesday night "MASH units" of medical students. I wanted the patients to know our faces and names. And I wanted the students to see where patients go when they are discharged from a free clinic.

We found a motley range of personalities. There were the nice guys and the jerks, the psychotics and the prostitutes, the hustlers and the entrepreneurs, and the accidental travelers lost in the layover.

And there was Elvis, as he was called by the other residents of the west-side Dungeon. He was a black gentleman in his late thirties, or maybe his early forties, a stranger to our clinic. A veteran of the Vietnam War, Elvis preferred to see doctors at the nearby VA hospital no matter how frequently we offered to provide him with care at Camillus.

Independent and reserved, he stood about six feet tall. He was friendly and strikingly articulate. Each time I visited his tattered spot in the Mudflats, I found him reading a different novel. Among his few possessions was a Dade County Public Library card, its edges curled from frequent use. Our conversations were lively and wide-ranging as we talked about books and current events and the twists of life. He was a great news analyst, a constant source of fascination for the med students, who realized Elvis was better read than most of them. Certainly he was better read than I. And I never stopped learning from Elvis, the literary prince under I-395. Never. I always looked forward to seeing him during my rounds under the bridge. Our friendship grew throughout the years with each Tuesday night chat.

One winter night, as the shadows of dusk settled down over the Mudflats, I parked my Jeep along the west side of North Miami Avenue. With four medical students in tow, I jumped out and climbed through an opening in the fence surrounding the underpass. As always, we stopped by to shoot the breeze with Elvis.

But things were different that night. We found Elvis unusually quiet, seemingly in pain. He lay sprawled atop his bed, an old spring mattress upon a shaky wooden

platform. This was his home, a soiled rectangle barely elevated above the rats and mud. He was surrounded by his
magazines and paperback books. Against the dust and
setting sun, his silhouette portrayed a suffering that went
beyond his poverty. Tired and wounded in this war, one
of the many Elvis had fought since Vietnam, he seemed to
be fighting for his life.

"Good evening, Elvis," I called out as I approached
his bed.

"Good evening, Doc," he replied between short
breaths.

"You don't look well tonight," I went on, taking his
wrist to check his pulse.

"The sides of my chest hurt, but at the VA today they
told me I was fine."

He said he was taking Vasotec to control his high
blood pressure. I knew the medication could make him
cough, but I was baffled by his chest pain.

"I'll see you after rounds," I promised once I got a
palpable pulse. I took a few steps with the students, then
turned again to Elvis.

"I'll pick you up and take you to the clinic, okay?"

For the first time since I had known Elvis, I heard
him say, "Okay."

Something was obviously wrong. That night, for the
first time, he finally took up our offer.

I led the students through the underpass, my pace a little quicker than usual. I had a nagging feeling that something was really wrong with Elvis. I just couldn't pinpoint what the hell it was. I found it nearly impossible to concentrate as we continued westward.

I called off the rounds earlier than usual, yards from the extreme western edge, the place that harbored the deepest recesses of poverty, drugs, and desperation. It was there, amid rat-infested heaps of trash, that young women lived in open cardboard boxes, trading their bodies for crack cocaine, subsisting on bits of food from the church vans. That night, they waved to us and we waved back. I explained that I was worried about Elvis and wanted to get him to the clinic as soon as possible.

There, on the west side, the law of the land was crack and violence. But that night, in that strange land, there was also compassion. A skinny young prostitute hurried to us with a plea: help Elvis, please. Her plea was echoed by the other young prostitutes we passed on the way back to Elvis's sickbed. For all the crap that surrounded me that night, the reaction from the young women parted the skies. A world away from the sacred tomes of medical school, crack hookers were teaching us a compelling lesson in empathy. It can survive the cruelest of elements and rise where you least expect it.

I had a gnawing sense of dread in my gut as I walked

back to Elvis. It was as if I faced an invisible rival who had already declared victory. I knew Elvis, condemned to a life no one should have to endure, was slipping away.

The students helped me lift him from his bed and carry him out of the Dungeon, through the hole in the fence, and into the back of my open Jeep. It was a five-minute ride back to the clinic. Together we helped Elvis down and carried him into the clinic.

In the first exam room, our nurse Ruth took his vital signs.

"He's breathing hard and his blood pressure is one ninety over one forty," Ruth anxiously reported.

"Pulse?" I asked.

"About one ten—and thready," she replied in a tone that reflected my own fears.

I walked into the exam room and stopped by Elvis's bed. He looked like hell, pale, sunken, and scared. I placed a stethoscope on his chest and listened to the irregular patterns of his heart and lungs. I palpated his belly, piecing together all the possible diagnoses. None were good. All were emergencies.

A medical student helped me hook him up to an EKG machine, a contraption that was probably as old as Elvis himself. We stared at the tracing, the fleeting assurance that his heart was still working. The blip patterns revealed only minimal signs of ischemia, lack of oxygen. Again, I checked his pulse. It was palpable, but weakening. Knowing his history of hypertension, I gave Elvis ten milligrams of nifedipine under the tongue to bring his blood pressure down. No more than three minutes later, I took his blood pressure again. This time it was 210 over 155. He looked worse, medically and emotionally. I wasn't feeling much better myself. I called Miami Fire Rescue. Elvis needed more than we had to offer.

We waited only moments, but it seemed an eternity. Elvis began to cough, shallow and painfully at first. Then, out of nowhere, his color worsened, his pallor turned ashen. His shallow cough became projectile, as clots and strings of bright-red blood flew forward each time he coughed. I tried in vain to stop a bleed that was coming from God knew where, all the while attempting to reassure him.

The paramedics burst in through the back door wearing vinyl gloves and pushing an orange stretcher, their metal toolbox clanging alongside them. They lifted Elvis onto the stretcher and jumped to action, getting his pulse and blood pressure, hooking him up to large-bore intravenous lines. As the clear fluid dripped from the IV, Elvis continued to cough up blood. The paramedics strapped him to the stretcher and quickly wheeled him out to the Fire Rescue truck. I ran alongside, trying to calm my friend and trying to calm myself, until I reached the truck.

Back in the fluorescent light of the clinic, homeless men and women packed the waiting room. But that night it was Elvis's struggle that consumed all my thoughts. I stood in the middle of the street in an almost surrealistic frenzy. The paramedics snapped the stretcher into place in the back of the truck. Elvis lay conscious, wired to monitors as the IV continued to drip. His aura radiated fear. I placed my hand on his shoulder and massaged it, trying to calm emotions I knew could not be calmed.

"Elvis, I'll see you at Jackson when I'm done here tonight," I told him. In my heart, I prayed that that would be true.

"Doc," Elvis whispered between coughs and labored breaths, "I don't think I'll make it." Again he coughed up blood.

"I'll see you there," I repeated, trying to convince Elvis and myself.

Twice before in my career as a physician I had heard patients tell me they were going to die. The first time, it was from a young woman in the emergency room of a small hospital in Puerto Plata, on the north coast of the Dominican Republic. I had never seen her before. A poor woman in her twenties, she described a pain in her belly that had intensified throughout the day. I examined her and found her vital signs stable, but her lower abdomen tender. Heeding her fear, I had her admitted to the hospital.

A similar incident occurred when I was a second-year resident at the VA hospital. One night during my rounds in the intensive care unit, a critically ill patient tapped my forearm and silently handed me a scrap of paper. I glanced down at the shaky letters. "I'm going to die," the note said.

One way or another, both of these patients had announced their deaths. Both were right.

But I couldn't accept the same message from Elvis.

As the Fire Rescue team pressed ahead, I returned to the other patients who waited in the clinic. I stopped at the first exam room. It was difficult to concentrate as Elvis's words rang in my head. Why? I pondered the gulf between my world and the world Elvis suffered in. Years before, I had crossed that gulf into that other place, where painful lessons awaited. I had memorized the names and faces and diseases. I had cleaned the wounds and filled the prescriptions. But what was it all for if I couldn't save this one life? What was the use? The crack fires still raged. The river of human misery kept flowing. The shit was all over the place. How could it be that a man like Elvis, who went to war for the United States, existed the way he did? It was beyond my comprehension.

I tried to bring my mind back to the exam room, to focus on the patient before me. He, too, was sick and needed attention. But suddenly I heard the clinic door swing open and a paramedic rush in.

"Elvis coded," he yelled.

I ran out to the truck and there lay my friend, with the mechanical thumper still compressing his chest. With every thump, he would bring up blood through the endotracheal tube and into the bag that was supposed to push oxygen into his lungs. There was blood everywhere, on Elvis and all over the truck. The monitor showed upward deflections only when the thumper pushed down on Elvis's chest.

"Open the Ringer's lactate," I instructed the paramedic. "Start the dopamine. Stop the thumper—do we have a pulse?"

"Nothing," he responded, his fingers pressed against the sides of Elvis's neck.

"Start the thumper and let me see the monitor," I told the paramedics.

Nothing, damn it, nothing, I thought. Elvis was dead, but I wasn't giving up. We were going to give him the full court press. I was determined to give this gentle soldier every chance at life.

We tried to save him for what seemed to be an eternity, although it was no more than fifteen minutes. I knew that the Fire Rescue team was simply following my orders, waiting for me to accept what everyone around me already knew. I realized it was not life but machines and drugs that were pumping through an already lifeless body. I took a deep breath.

"Stop." I relented, giving my last medical order for Elvis. "Call it."

The monitor showed a flat line. It was a Tuesday, a cool winter night in Miami outside the Camillus Health Concern on Northeast First Avenue. It was the night Elvis, literary prince of the Mudflats, died, a homeless friend gone home.

I stood at the edge of his stretcher in a numb state, contemplating my friend's face, his hands, his final moments of solitude. I remembered the tuberculosis patient in the ICU in bed 9 at Jackson Memorial, the one whose death had launched my journey into this abyss years ago. But as I faced this death, everything seemed different. I had none of the angry drive of the early days. Instead, I slumped in defeat. I could make no sense of what had just happened. Unlike the first death, this one rang no wake-up calls. What was the damned point?

Like my patients at Camillus, I, too, longed for refuge from the streets.

All

Alone

It's bad, ain't it?

—Emergency-room patient

SOMETIMES I THOUGHT PLUNGING full-force into my residency at the hospital, where we could save lives, would take me away from the horrors I was witnessing under the bridges. The enemy, I thought back then, lurked only outside.

But of course, that wasn't true. The homeless, I quickly learned, were simply the visual reality of poverty. Invisible and sprawling, poverty extended its tenebrous reach well beyond the bridges. In the late 1980s and into the '90s, Miami was the fourth-poorest city in the country, a fact affirmed with each poor family I encountered. Years into my Camillus work, I would read the grimmest statistics in the eyes of undocumented immigrant children at another free clinic we opened, in Little Havana, at the San Juan Bosco Catholic Church. And when we opened up clinics in the South Dade migrant-labor camps in the wake of Hurricane Andrew in 1992, I would again detect that invisible barrier that fences in the disadvantaged population we serve.

So it didn't matter where I was—the hospital, the streets, the camps, or the clinics. The tragedies were the same; only, the human suffering was made more acute by poverty. ✍

In the constant grind of the ER, the patterns repeated themselves hour upon hour. The crush of patients. Their languishing upon stiff plastic chairs. Their stories of hardship. But even these repetitions carried no numbing side effects, no analgesic balm for the residents who worked the unit. That's because diseases don't walk in by themselves. They are attached to mothers and grandfathers and sweet infants. They come with painful tangents—a home that burned down, a lover who violently lashed out, a father who walked away. And sometimes they come disguised as prophets of death.

A poor woman and her teenage daughter made it into the ER after a fourteen-hour wait. But the three interns on call that night were all busy with other patients. Her assigned physician, one of the interns pulling the thirty-six-hour shift, had hours to go before he could even look at her. I was on call that night, responsible for supervising those three interns, but I wasn't on the floor at the moment. I had admitted twelve new patients, and it was my turn to sleep. I had just laid my head on the pillow in the hospital's nearby Memorial Hall when my beeper went off.

"Call the ER. Call the ER," the beeper crackled.

They said they needed me to work up a new patient. It was 4 A.M. I rolled out of bed and splashed some water on my face, and tried to piece together the fragments of information I had on this patient. She was thirty-eight years old. She came in because her belly kept growing. Otherwise, she was losing weight so quickly her clothes no longer fit. Of all the diagnoses I could come up with, not one had a good ending. She had fluid in her belly— lots of it. It could be from liver disease, I thought—but then again, those patients generally gain weight. It could be her kidneys. Or it could be cancer.

I hadn't even met this woman and already I was handing her the worst possible diagnosis. I tried to clear my thoughts as I stepped into the cool night air and walked briskly one and a half blocks to the ER door. The waiting room was packed, as usual. Four in the morning or four in the afternoon, it was always Grand Central Station in there.

I walked past rows of people fidgeting or trying to sleep on the plastic chairs, past the night nurses at the triage desk. I wove between randomly placed stretchers, some of them covered in soiled sheets, upon which patients waited. I could see some of them tossing and turning in discomfort, and others simply resting silently as IV tubes arched gracefully from plastic bags, dripping either clear saline or a yellow cocktail into their veins. There were even more gurneys beyond a set of double doors that led into the medical emergency room. I turned a corner and peered down the walkway to the end. There stood a tall girl next to a stretcher that cradled her mother. The two of them stood out even at a distance, a sad-faced adolescent waiting calmly amid the chaos of what was the busiest emergency room in America at the time.

The girl's mother would be my patient until the resident I was covering for returned to rounds in a few hours.

I contemplated the poignant portrait of mother and daughter. Somehow I knew the story would be worse than I had imagined. I walked to the desk and picked up the woman's chart. The ER crew had done a thorough workup, including an ultrasound of her abdomen. It showed large amounts of ascites (fluid in the belly) as well as a mass, a tumor in the pelvis that looked like an ovarian carcinoma. As I flipped the pages on the clipboard, I glanced down the walkway. The girl, barely into her teens, leaned against the wall, clearly exhausted. This was not going to be easy. Even without talking to the patient, I knew the diagnosis would be traumatic. I took a deep breath and started down the corridor. I extended my hand and introduced myself to the daughter.

"How old are you?" I asked.

"Thirteen," she replied, her voice laced with a Southern drawl. In the same breath she delivered a heartbreaking story: "We just left this hospital last month. My baby brother died here after surgery for his heart."

What else was in store for this young lady? I turned to look at her mother, who was smiling although she was visibly in pain. Though I'd seen many sad cases in my career, I cannot tell you how difficult it was for me to hold back the tears this time. I knew they were waiting for encouraging words from their doctor, a little good news after the shock of losing a baby. But I had none to give them. I pulled up a plastic chair and listened to the entire story.

"I'm sorry they woke you up," the mother said in a half whisper, casting her eyes downward. "You see, the reason we came here is we moved from the Carolinas, because we brought my sick baby boy for surgery in his heart, right here in this same hospital."

I didn't understand why they came to Miami, a place where, it turns out, they knew no one, for the child's heart surgery, but I didn't want to ask too many nonmedical questions. I simply let her speak.

"We spent all our money on him, every last penny, and now he's dead."

We both remained silent as I reached for her hand with both of mine.

"You see," she went on between shallow, labored breaths, "I don't have family here. I didn't want to leave my daughter alone in our trailer, where we live."

"No, no," I agreed, "you were right to bring her."

I told her I would do my best to take care of them. She tried to force some enthusiasm into her voice.

"How long will I be here, Doctor?"

By now it was nearly 5 A.M. At 8 A.M. a whole new shift of doctors would take over her case. I feared she might get lost in the rush of new cases. I had three hours to be kind, to make her comfortable—and to give her the worst news of her life. I never answered her last question, and she never asked it again. I turned and asked the daughter to go sit down in a nearby waiting area, so I could examine her mother. I explained to the patient I'd have to do an abdominal paracentesis, a procedure to tap the belly with a needle to remove the fluid. That way, I explained, she could breathe easier and we could make a more precise diagnosis. I asked if she had any questions. She said her only concern was her daughter.

She never asked about her illness. She knew. She knew better than all of science—perhaps not the cell type or the pathogenesis of her tumor, but she understood the language of her weakening body. To save her son she had lost almost everything, except her daughter. Now she knew it was her daughter who would lose her.

I walked to the rear of the ER to get the equipment I needed and brought it back to the stretcher. I lowered the back of the cot so that the patient could lie down flat. The fluid in her belly pressed up against her diaphragm, shortening her breath. I swabbed an area of her abdomen with reddish-brown Betadine to sterilize it, wiping it gently with an alcohol pad. I slid a small needle just under the skin, injecting just enough lidocaine to numb the nerves on the skin, then a little more to numb the tissue below it.

I thought, If only I had something to numb the

greater pain of her small family, to ease the shock her daughter would feel in just a short time.

As I waited for the local anesthesia to take effect, I talked to her about her son, the baby who had died after repeated open-heart surgeries. She told me she'd had hope at first, but then only desperation as she watched him wither away. She talked about her daughter, her greatest blessing.

"You know, Doc, it's just me and my girl now," she said. "And it's just me to take care of her—there's no one else down here."

I brought a gloved finger toward my lips to signal "Hush." Then I introduced a large-bore needle into her abdominal cavity. The numbing shots had worked—she felt only the decompression of her belly as the maroon-colored fluid was sucked through the needle into the tubing and down into glass bottles. One look at the fluid confirmed the diagnosis I dreaded. I was now sure it was malignant—nothing else looks like that. Yes, she had cancer. Yes, it was probably metastatic. No, there wasn't much we could do except tap her belly so that she could breathe a little better. We would also offer a debulking surgery and some toxic high-dose chemotherapy.

I had removed about seven liters of cancerous fluid from her abdomen. I stood up and snapped off my gloves. It was seven-fifteen in the morning. Soon I'd be home. But this family was a long way from home, and a long way from comfort. May God bless them, I prayed as I stepped away. I looked for her doctor, the young intern I was supervising. I wanted to talk to him before he got to the patient. I found him and pulled him aside and explained the case with all the medical jargon that makes a diagnosis seem so separate from the human being it concerns. Then it was time for the real conversation. I escorted him to a separate hallway outside the ER radiology area. I began to explain how serious a dilemma was on our hands.

"This situation requires the most intense sensitivity you can imagine, and more," I said.

"I understand, Joe, no problem," he quickly replied.

"Listen, for God's sake, don't let her daughter go to a foster home," I went on. "Get them both back to the Carolinas, North, South, wherever the hell they're from. Get them back to wherever the rest of the family is."

I was tired, emotionally drained, as we started our walk back to the ER, where I would introduce him to the patient and then deliver the diagnosis.

"Feeling better?" I asked her.

"Yeah, Doc, and I can breathe, too," she answered with a half smile. Seven liters of fluid out of her abdomen, she could now take a deep breath as she sat up. She seemed better prepared to handle what was coming next than was I.

"It's bad, ain't it?" She cast her eyes downward again.

"It looks that way," I said softly. "We still have to wait on the pathology, though." I hoped that would offer a glimmer of hope, unrealistic as it was.

"Thanks," she murmured, her smile fading.

I followed her eyes toward her daughter, now asleep in a plastic chair against the wall. She seemed so blissfully removed from the nightmare of her waking hours.

"How do you want us to tell your daughter?" I asked her.

Don't worry, she told us, she would handle it.

The intern spoke up. "We'll get you a good social worker and get you back home."

He and I walked over to the girl. I tapped her on the shoulder to wake her up. The intern grabbed a container of orange juice and a cellophane-wrapped muffin from another patient's tray and handed it to her.

"Good morning," I said. "Anything else we can get you?"

"No, thank you," she replied courteously.

"You know, we made your mom a little skinnier," I offered.

She gazed up with sad hazel eyes, eyes that revealed a child's vulnerable edges, yet an unexplained inner strength. They were eyes too young to be dimmed by the torments they witnessed. Momentarily, I was lost in the girl's gentle stare. I let my memory go deep into her gaze. But where was I going back to? Whose eyes were these now? The eyes that stared back belonged to a boy, a child who was once also alone in the world. ⤿

His name was Jean Paul. He was a Haitian boy I had met in 1983, when I was an intern on the north coast of the Dominican Republic. I first saw him in the dim, rustic emergency room of the hospital in Puerto Plata, in a hallway where the sick waited upon a slanted wooden bench under a single, unshaded fifty-watt bulb.

Jean Paul was a small skinny boy, hunched over. His abdominal wall bore a mosaic of infected, open wounds. His back was frozen in a permanent forward arch. To see his face, I had to bend down and look up at him. He was feverish and his belly was rock hard. Yet even though he had every reason to cry and complain, he didn't. He smiled.

Barely nine years old, Jean Paul was a slave boy, invisible to Dominican eyes. His journey to this strange land had begun some years earlier, in the middle of the night. His uncle came and snatched Jean Paul from his mother's home outside Port-au-Prince and forced him across the border. The uncle sold the boy into slavery, to be a laborer in the Dominican sugarcane fields, but not before a mob of border guards brutalized the child. The guards beat Jean Paul so badly that they shattered his spinal cord in several places. Without medical attention, the boy's vertebral column fused into an arch that would never allow him to stand up straight or lift his head.

He lived in absolute squalor, in a cramped, thatch-roofed commune of sugarcane workers who slept on a dirt floor. On stormy nights, rats scurried through the maze of bodies. His chores were worse than his living conditions. Since the hunchbacked boy was no longer useful as a sugarcane cutter, he was forced to carry the buckets of water to the other workers. In other words, he became a slaves' slave.

His presenting medical problems were dreadful. Out of his abcesses grew a penicillin-resistant organism. In other words, no simple or stock antibiotic could help him. The boy had no money or family. The hospital had few resources to offer him. The medication he needed would cost $10 a day for a twenty-one-day course. That was more than he could ever hope to earn in a year.

So, every day before going to the hospital for rounds, I would stop by a private pharmacy and pick up the antibiotics that would be given intravenously to Jean Paul. After the first week and a half, he seemed to be doing better, his progress reflected in his easy laugh. His sharp, cheerful disposition began to surface. He was a brilliant boy who maneuvered in and out of three languages, Haitian Creole, Spanish, and a little English. In spite of the horrors of his life, his spirit was unsinkable, as was his desire to learn and to play.

Over the following two months we became pretty good friends. My wife, Janus, went out and bought him some clothes, shoes, and toys. He would keep these, his most valued possessions, under his pillow, sharing the toys with the other sick children.

When he got better, we began to take him to the outdoor restaurant next to the hospital, a big oceanfront café where a rhythm band played. There he had his first pizza and hamburger. Our favorite, though, was the Dominican house special, *chicharrones de pollo* and *patacones*—fried chicken bits and double-fried, smashed green plantains.

I tried to get Jean Paul back to his family in Haiti, but the Dominican government didn't make it easy. Since Jean Paul had been smuggled into the country, he didn't exist. He needed documents—papers that looked a lot like dollars. Even if I did pay off someone to get him out, where would I send him? Besides, my rotation in Puerto Plata was coming to an end. In two weeks I would be off to Janico, a mountain village in the Cibao. Luckily, a priest who used to visit the hospital agreed to care for Jean Paul.

About eight months later, while I was making rounds in another Dominican hospital, I got a telephone call from Puerto Plata. It was from a sweet-voiced nun with cheerful news to deliver. Jean Paul had been reunited with his family in Port-au-Prince. He had asked her to call me. This gifted boy, once broken and stranded, was no longer alone. In many ways he had been my teacher, a child who led me through the lessons of keeping hope alive in the most dismal conditions. His story had a happy ending. ✧

Back in America, in the eyes of a poor thirteen-year-old girl, I could see only pain. No happy ending in sight. As I walked back to the desk to finish my notes, I watched the girl stand up and go to her mother. Somehow the commotion of the emergency room, the changing of the shifts, the chronic background din all seemed muted, suspended in another dimension. For the moment, I was totally enveloped in one family's tragedy. I looked over and caught the mother's glance as she wiped away tears. Then mother and daughter hugged each other. I walked away, trying with all my power not to look back.

It was 8 A.M. and my work was done. I left the emergency room by the same path I had entered. Gurneys were scattered everywhere. Patients were beginning to wake up as the sun filtered in. I waved good-bye to the morning shift of nurses and walked out the door, into the sun. I couldn't shake that final scene of mother and daughter hugging. I whispered a prayer for both of them, for the mother who might soon rejoin her baby son and for the daughter who was destined to say good-bye.

No, the hopeless cases were not confined to the streets. They were all over the wards. The only good news for this poor mother was that she got in the door in the first place. Others weren't that lucky.

Men

in Suits

～

The public hospital isn't free just because of [the patients'] inability to pay.

—Jackson Memorial
Hospital administrator

Those patients who were lucky enough—or insured enough—to be admitted at the hospital were called "hits" in the slang of the residents. Those who didn't get in were called "misses." These were the poor who were sent back home—or back to the street—

untreated. These were the victims of the enemy that lurked inside the hospital.

To an overworked resident scrambling to save a life, the enemy quickly became the jerk in the suit who would seek some microscopic disclaimer in the law to prevent a poor patient from being admitted. We were the county's only "public" hospital, that quintessential reflection of America's beneficence, where the bottom line is signed off by an accountant. We knew the enemy well. We didn't realize that this enemy foreshadowed something that expanded well beyond the corridors of JMH, a plague extending throughout health care. This enemy would exemplify all that is wrong with medicine, the HMO profiteers, the managed-care fiascos, the tightening embargo against the poor.

As frontline doctors in the ER, our unwritten policy was this: Get that sick patient admitted one way or another. Then, and only then, did we have the power to heal. An administrator could not discharge a patient who had crossed the bureaucratic threshold. Therefore the trick was getting these patients admitted. Sometimes it took fudging the story to save a life.

The administrators had lots of tricks of their own. Sometimes they would demand large deposits from poor patients, threaten them with liens on their homes or whatever possessions they had. Quite a comforting exercise, as you can imagine, for a sick person of little means. Our battles, therefore, were not only against illness, but also against ill will.

Then again, some patients beat the administrators without any help from us.

I remember one pleasant gentleman, an uninsured patient from Chicago, who came to the ER with melena—digested blood in the stool, suggesting bleeding in the stomach. Sitting on a stretcher in the exam room, he was pale and tired. I introduced myself and asked him why he was there, although I knew. I had read the chart. It said he had undergone extensive bowel resections for recurrent bleeds from arterial malformations. He was telling me about his surgeries when the door to the tiny exam room blew open, nearly hitting my back. The administrator on call pranced in and pulled me out of the room. He rattled off a litany of reasons why this patient would not be admitted:

"One, he's a nonresident. Two, he's hemodynamically stable. His blood pressure is fine, his pulse is fine. Doctor, it's not a life-or-death issue."

I wanted to hit him. But I came back with the medical history, reason enough for admission.

"Oh come on, this patient is bleeding," I argued.

"Fine. We'll just have to call your attending," he threatened.

"Fine, go ahead," I came back, knowing our attending would never send home a bleeding patient. "He's a physician. He cares about the patient."

So the administrator once again pranced into the exam room and went to work.

In a condescending tone, he threatened the patient. "So, this is the diagnosis? Then if you're gonna stay here, we're gonna need a $5,000 deposit. Now!"

Well, from the administrative perspective, he picked the wrong time to throw a fit in the ER. His poor, harassed target began to get nauseous. Still, the administrator persisted. Even when he saw the patient struggle to get off the stretcher, he blabbed on. The patient managed to get to the sink, but not before he vomited bright-red blood all over the administrator. The patient was admitted without the deposit. He survived and did well. I can't say the same for the administrator's suit. But that night, we won two battles, one against a poor man's illness, another against the enemy. ✐

Trust me when I tell you this administrator was a small fish in an ocean of sharks, his demeanor indicative of a greater rot. At their wood-paneled level, administrators and trustees carved up the fat, indulged one another in quiet perks, covered one another's behind. Meanwhile, too many poor people with critical medical needs languished on waiting lists. Other very sick patients were forced to walk away, unable to pay the steep deposits. The divide between the hospital's powerful administration and its poorest constituents grew wider each day.

I remember the most blatant example, in October 1991. Just one month after Miami-Dade voters approved a half-cent sales tax to help Jackson take care of the county's poor, the hospital chiefs decided to spend $250,000 in public funds to renovate the boardroom. Not only would they expand their west-wing facility; they would jazz it up with a $14,000 mahogany table and a $28,000 set of leather-covered chairs. That was until the press found out about it, of course. Amid a firestorm of public criticism, the hospital brass moonwalked out of the original plan, settling on a scaled-back, privately funded version.

Still, the damage had been done, the arrogant nature of the beast revealed. Well before the story broke, the boardroom had already been gutted and prepped for construction. Hospital chiefs argued they needed the space to accommodate a newly expanded Public Health Trust, the hospital's governing board. But the math seemed preposterous: spending a quarter of a million dollars to accommodate six new board members broke down to more than $40,000 per new trustee.

Then again, these were no ordinary characters. Take, for instance, the flashy S&L chairman who arrived for board meetings in a stretch Mercedes-Benz limo. While he sat on the board, applauded in society cliques for his philanthropy, he was amassing a dizzying level of opulence— thanks not so much to his savings as to his "loans."

Eventually he would be outdazzled by federal regulators. In the end, he got slapped with a hundred-count felony indictment and was later convicted on sixty-eight racketeering and bank-fraud charges. At a separate trial, he pled guilty to twenty-nine securities-fraud counts. In 1994, he was sentenced to eleven years in federal prison for looting the S&L and forcing taxpayers to put up millions in bailout funds.

But in his heyday he was Miami's favorite big spender. Limo here. Private jet there. Oh, yes, and a $7 million yacht equipped with a marble fireplace, silk wallpaper, and gold-leaf ceilings. When the government men finally descended on the S&L, they nearly went berserk. The S&L chairman had furnished his corporate quarters with mahogany floors, gold-plated sinks, and a dining room appointed by Tiffany & Co. And he had lined the S&L's executive suite with a $30 million collection of old master paintings. "On loan" to the chairman's private mansion: the pièce de résistance, a $13.2 million Rubens.

As a member of the Public Health Trust, he must

have found kindred spirits at Jackson, where corporate sins seemed to mount by the week. The unflappable hospital president set off alarms from the day he was hired. Before he had even settled into his new office, he got into trouble for asking an influential board member for help in obtaining a housing loan. So, off the bat, the president was owing favors. Still, most board members supported him just the same. They gave him a $40,000 raise his second year on the job, making the head of Dade's hospital for the poor the highest-paid official in the county.

I guess you could say the president spread the wealth. He promoted aides, sparing few expenses. After he hired a $125,000-a-year chief operating officer in 1989, he approved unlimited travel expenses. That year, the debt-ridden hospital paid more than $12,000 for this exec to fly home to Dallas nearly every weekend, or for his family to visit him in Miami. But that's not all. That same year, Jackson picked up the travel expenses of yet another executive, a new vice president, whose family lived in New Orleans.

The tens of thousands spent on these travel sprees was made more egregious by the fact that Jackson was $30 million in the red. Outraged, the *Miami Herald,* in a July 1989 editorial, slammed hospital chiefs for the "outlandish" payments: "This excessive tapping of the public till would be indefensible even if JMH weren't in a constant fiscal crisis. But in light of an impending $30 million deficit and the lavish raises given a dozen aides whom [the JMH president] promoted to vice presidencies, this largess goes beyond indefensibility to become insolence."

The scandal didn't end there. That year, an internal audit revealed some of these payments came from a deep discretionary fund operated by the hospital president. In blatant violation of donor restrictions and Public Health Trust policies, the president had created a substantial President's Trust Fund, merging $180,000 dollars from smaller accounts. Included were funds donated by boosters and hospital employees for planting trees and historic restorations. Yet the president got off with a mild scolding: he was forced to return less than one-third of the cash to the original funds.

Although several Public Health Trust members questioned the president's mounting scandals, the majority rose to his defense. Undeterred by his detractors, he plunged ahead into murkier streams. The following year, the public learned he had been working as a paid consultant to a national supply company that was doing business with Jackson. While the president accepted fees and travel expenses from the Indiana-based Hill-Rom firm, his hospital had purchased some $150,000 in products from the supplier.

Et cetera. Et cetera.

Meanwhile, at the height of all this executive largess,

a hotel maid named Anne Marie Lane was denied medical care at Jackson simply because she didn't have a $200 deposit. At Jackson, if you weren't a resident of the county and didn't have a life-or-death medical situation, the rule was you had to pay, regardless of your ability to do so. The deposit was based on a percentage of your estimated total bill. Lane was turned away even though she had a fibrous tumor the size of a basketball in her uterus. The reason she couldn't pay the deposit was that she had been unable to work for months at a time. She was in too much pain. Finally, after the story was made public, a surgeon from a private hospital volunteered to remove the tumor.

Jackson officials seemed to have an explanation for everything. One administrator replied this way when a *Miami Herald* reporter questioned the public hospital's cash-for-care policy: "We won't deny needed medical care that we define as emergency care. But beyond that, we will ask for deposits from everybody. What we're trying to do here is to let people know the public hospital isn't free just because of their inability to pay."

And all along I had thought this was the hospital for those who couldn't pay.

Outside JMH, the outrage was building. How could the county's only public hospital discriminate against the poor and uninsured so openly? In 1991, a couple of would-be patients filed a complaint with the U.S. Department of

Health and Human Services after they were denied critically needed care at Jackson just because they couldn't pay
the deposit.

The entire situation was growing out of control. On
the streets and under the bridges, the extremes of poverty
churned out an increasing number of medical emergencies. But where were these patients to go?

The war continued. And so did we, albeit battle weary,
our drive recharged by even the smallest victory. I feel
obliged to say there were also beacons of humanity to guide
us through the bureaucratic labyrinth. Chief among them
was our attending physician, Dr. Bernard Elser, head of the
ER. As he watched the poor and homeless pack into the
emergency room each night, he came up with an unofficial
remedy. He knew most of these patients would be discharged back to the streets, tired and hungry. So he transformed a small corner inside the ER into a makeshift unit
for rest and restorative meals. "Bernie's Nursing Home" we
called the collection of eight or so stretchers. Dr. Elser knew
that if we kept a patient too long in the ER, we had to feed
them. His holding zone guaranteed a homeless patient at
least one meal before facing the streets again. ⟋

The conspirators against the poor were as diverse as the
poor themselves. Yes, they wore natty suits and warmed

the leather chairs of the boardroom. But they also wore blue uniforms and staged city-ordered sweeps in public parks and underpasses. Miami police carried out sweeps with the vengeance of an exterminator. To the cops on "vagrant" detail, the homeless were nothing more than pests. The police seemed to prefer the old slash-and-burn strategies of war, rousting people as they slept in public areas like Bicentennial Park and Lummus Park, destroying their possessions, handcuffing them, and carting them off to jail. During one notorious night raid at Downtown's Lummus Park, police descended upon a cluster of homeless people as they slept and set fire to their possessions, which included clothing, identification documents, medicine, and a Bible. Such destruction was comparable to sweeping away someone's home. The shopping-cart clutter reflected in the mirrored glasses of a Miami cop often represented the only worldly possessions of a homeless man or woman. That was it: that was their kitchen, their bathroom, their den, their world.

The brutality would intensify whenever it was time for Miami to shine in the national spotlight: Pope John Paul II's 1987 visit, the Miami Grand Prix, the annual Orange Bowl parade, and, of course, the big NBA splash. On these occasions, the city didn't hesitate to spend the big bucks—the ones it would never dare spend on social services—on landscaping and street cleaning. And of course, sprucing up the public spaces always meant clearing out the "undesirables," even if it meant bulldozing encampments. In their zeal to tidy up the house, city authorities trampled all over the Constitution.

In 1988, the same year the Miami Arena opened its doors to the NBA, the American Civil Liberties Union sued the city of Miami on behalf of three homeless clients in a class action representing some six thousand homeless individuals. The ACLU charged that the city's strong-arm sweeps against the homeless violated a most basic, inalienable constitutional right: the right to freely engage in essential, life-sustaining activities. In other words, the homeless bathed and cooked and slept in the park because they had nowhere else to bathe and cook and sleep.

The actions of the city against the homeless were blatantly cruel and easily proved by an abundance of evidence. In internal city memos, city officials detailed the raids and used disparaging and ominous terms to characterize the most tattered members of their constituency. City Hall and police documents spoke matter-of-factly about "vagrant control" and "derelicts" and "half-naked, half-drunk bums" and "other undesirables creating nuisance."

During the trial, I was asked to testify on behalf of the homeless. For my testimony, I showed slides of the Mudflats and delivered a lecture I often used when speaking to medical students. I spoke about the medical consequences of the city's inappropriate social policies. I talked about the soaring rate of tuberculosis, how the cases among the homeless in Miami exceeded those in Haiti.

It would take well over ten years for the case to be settled—in favor of the homeless. In the summer of 1998, the city officially offered restitution to individuals whose civil rights had been violated through unlawful arrests, destruction of personal property, and other acts against the homeless that took place during the sweeps of the parks and streets. ↜

The conspirators against the poor also carried clipboards and sales cases and fanned out underneath the highways, seeking converts to the evangelism of health-maintenance organizations. In their generic sweep, the HMOs came to represent doctors and medical entrepreneurs who loathe medicine but love a fast buck. And it seemed as if our state and federal governments were too willing to sell the poor and elderly down the river to the profiteers. The more I learned about HMOs, the more they reminded me of my parents' stories of communism: The party leaders live high on the hog. The proletariat is not regarded as a composite of individuals with unique concerns, but as a monolith to be disrespected.

HMO recruiters stalked poor people, swept the un-

derpasses, infiltrated food-stamp lines. They offered everything from free diapers to gift certificates to blood-pressure
screenings. Making $50 to $200 for each patient they
signed up, some sales agents even handed out $10,000
life-insurance policies.

The payoff for the HMO industry was enormous. Patients—or "lives," in HMO lingo—meant bucks. For
every patient recruited, the HMO would get from $100 to
$700 a month from Tallahassee and Washington—even if
the individual never came in for care. It was called "capitation," the funneling of tax dollars to the HMOs. It meant
the HMO was now responsible for each funded patient.
But in reality, it meant the HMO would treat only those
who figured out how to get there (this was back when
"HMO" wasn't simply a term to describe a type of managed care, but actually referred to a freestanding facility
where patients would try to receive medical care) and
how to play the system. Too many poor patients had no
information, no transportation. Lured by slick promises
and giveaways, they'd sign away their benefits, only to
find out later that the HMO was really fifty miles away, in
the next county. But the public bucks kept pouring in as
HMOs kept profiting off leagues of poor, uninformed patients without having to answer to anyone. What can you
say about a system that refers to their patients as "lives"
and any medical expense as "loss ratio"?

Needless to say, it was open terrain for hucksters with their empty promises and forgery schemes. And needless to say, sooner or later the predators would turn up at Camillus, where they would make their pitch in the waiting room—until we kicked them out, of course.

They were in essence bottom feeders. They would stop at nothing. More than once they followed our AIDS van, the medical unit that delivers care to homeless HIV-infected patients. You see, if the patient had AIDS, chances were they also had Medicaid. Sniffing the opportunity, the recruiters descended upon the Mudflats with chicken dinners, food coupons, even feminine-hygiene products. Too many times, they'd leave with a stack of conquests. The patients, of course, kept coming to Camillus.

When we discovered the predatory tactics, we were steamed. It didn't take long to figure out that our patients were being used for ill gains. I heard it from the homeless mothers at the clinic, the AIDS patients in the Mudflats, the veterans on the street. Another revolution began swirling in my head, except this time I wasn't driving on I-95. I was wandering underneath it.

But even in the face of this rampant disregard of medical ethics, there was little we could do. The HMOs and their operatives were protected by law. We could, however, speak out, write op-ed pieces, blow the cover off the process. We started taking names. At the clinic, we began keeping records of all the women and children, documenting how many had been recruited by HMOs, and why they weren't receiving medical attention where they had signed up.

After almost twelve months and countless other run-ins with the HMO stalkers, we had enough ammo to fire the first salvos. A complex picture had emerged. Some of our poor and homeless mothers were undocumented immigrants with at least one child born in the United States. That American child made them eligible for Medicaid, and vulnerable to the pitches of the recruiters. These mothers had little or no transportation. Most of the time, they couldn't get to their designated HMO. Other times, they found the wait was too long or the available appointments didn't fit their work schedule.

At Camillus, we offered pediatric care and a room for child care. The HMOs, the women told us, had no day care. Rarely did they allow joint appointments for mother and child. The undocumented mothers were afraid to complain for fear of *"la migra,"* the immigration officials. The documented and U.S.-born mothers didn't know they could complain. Imagine a system called "health maintenance" that doesn't even begin to take into account that a single mother, who must work to support her kids, can't afford to take a day off work, risk less pay, just to get a simple physical.

The Medicaid HMOs sprang up shortly after we opened our Camillus clinic, after the commercial HMOs refused to take Florida's Medicaid patients. In exchange, Tallahassee made it easier for Medicaid HMOs to get licensed, giving them breaks on the usual financial requirements. In the beginning, there were three Medicaid HMOs with nine thousand members. Ten years later, there were nearly fifty times the number of poor patients enrolled in a mushrooming system of Medicaid HMOs, and hundreds of millions of dollars in the profiteers' coffers.

If only that money had been used to take care of the poor, it might have lightened Camillus's burgeoning caseload. While the for-profits were rolling in the dough, we had to hustle like my friend Ice for spare change.

Pennies

from

Heaven

~

We've been following your work and we
wish to help you financially.

—Anonymous caller

I CONFESS, I HAVE NEVER BEEN A businessman, but as my clinic work evolved, I was beginning to feel like one. I was beginning to detest the economic aspects of providing ever-increasing amounts of health care to the homeless. After just a few years, our clinic was bursting at the seams. The things we once could do on blood, guts, and borrowed goods seemed costly and complex as our patient population multiplied. How could we keep up with the patient load if we did not increase the medical staff? How could we realistically increase the staff without paying some salaries? Where was I supposed to get the money? I didn't have a clue. And frankly, I didn't have the desire to learn the math.

Sometimes I thought we could solve the problem by staying small, true to our roots. But the statistics weren't cooperating—nor were the public health facilities. I began to wonder how I got to this place of scarce dollars and decreasing sense.

Then one day as I was walking through the clinic kitchen, I found some students from St. Thomas Aquinas High School serving the lunch line. Their chaperon, the phys-ed coach, recognized me and came to say hello.

"You're Joe Greer, aren't you?" he asked.

"Yes, sir," I replied. "Welcome to Camillus."

"I've been here before, years ago, when I was a coach at St. Brendan's," he went on.

He didn't look familiar, although I remembered St. Brendan's quite well. That was the high school my sister Chichi went to.

"I used to be Chichi's coach," he said. "We'd come here a lot."

His words stunned me. My little sister had been to Camillus? She had walked through these same corridors before I even knew the place existed?

"Chichi was here?" I asked in disbelief.

"Yes, she was, a lot," he repeated. "She used to love to volunteer here. The people loved her. By the way, I was sorry to hear about her passing—"

I stopped him. "Please, don't apologize. You've just given me something wonderful. Thank you."

There I was, elbow deep in rising bureaucracy, feeling increasingly detached from the core reasons that had first led me through the shelter door. Suddenly, as if by angelic guidance, came this reminder: I was there for Chichi. And now I knew that in some very powerful way, she was there, too. It was her spirit that moved throughout that clinic, that kept it functioning amid the chaos, that kept me there in the worst of times. The coach's words couldn't have come at a better moment. I needed the fuel to go on, even if it meant braving the world of funding and grants.

In 1987, I served as chief medical resident at the Veterans Administration medical center, mastering the administrative and political skills that tenure teaches. The VA job also put me in a good position to promote the cause of the homeless. As chief resident, it was my duty to arrange all of the medical staff's conferences and secure sponsorship for them. That meant somebody else always paid for breakfast or lunch. That also meant pharmaceutical freebies, courtesy of the sponsors, who wanted to push their wares on our batch of new doctors. I saw this as an opportunity. I would allow the companies to promote their products if they agreed to donate all the samples to Camillus. They agreed. My one-year term at the VA would prove quite profitable for the clinic.

At around the same time, Camillus caught another much-needed break. One day, as I was making rounds through the second floor of the hospital, my pager went off.

"Dr. Greer, long-distance call," the voice crackled.

When I dialed the number, I got an unfamiliar voice and a greeting I was not ready for: "Hello, Dr. Greer, I represent a nonprofit group. We've been following your work and we wish to help you financially."

"Yeah, right," I replied with a laugh, waiting for the punch line. "What can I do for you?"

"No, truly, we want to help you," the caller insisted. "First, it's important you understand there's a new congressional act called the McKinney Act. It allocates money for homeless causes. You should apply. There's a deadline. Apply early."

The caller still hadn't given me his name, but already he was giving me the key to Camillus's future.

"I represent a new private group formed to help fi-

nance health care for homeless people. We want to work
with you. We'll be in touch soon."

That group, I later learned, was called Comic Relief.
But the call was no joke. The caller gave me his name at
the end of the conversation, but I must confess I don't remember what it was. Still, our conversation opened up a
new world for me. I had not heard of the landmark congressional act or the compelling story that had led to its
recent passage, in 1988. It was championed by Stewart B.
McKinney, an unconventional congressman from Con-
necticut, a moderate, so-called gypsy-moth Republican,
who went against the conservative grain and rallied for
homeless rights. He was so passionate about his proposed
legislation that he actually spent the night on a Capitol
Hill heat grate to raise awareness. He died that same year
of AIDS-related causes.

In addition to calling our attention to this new
source of funding, Comic Relief was willing to come to
Miami and help us put on benefit shows. They were a hit
from the start. Our first performance, hosted by local
comedian David Glickman, raised $14,000, enough to
finish outfitting the clinic's expanded space, the one designed and built by my friend Carlos Santeiro. Due to
lack of funds, it had stood empty for more than a year.
(And our stash of goods from the remodeled VA had gone
only so far.)

Comic Relief, the phenomenon made popular by producer Bob Zmuda and comics Whoopi Goldberg, Robin Williams, and Billy Crystal, became an important lifeline for Camillus. Over the years, the group has raised more than $750,000 for us and advocated our cause in Washington, D.C. They've also brought big names to our town, people like comedian Paul Rodriguez, who joined me on rounds under the bridge.

It was Alina Perez-Stable who would take the lead and write our first grant application for funds under the McKinney Act. We knew what we wanted to say, and unlike other applicants, we weren't asking them to fund an idea or an exploration, but a proven commitment, a clinic that had been operating now for four years.

A few days before the grant proposal was due, I got a taste of the turf battles that loomed ahead. The director of a (now defunct) nonprofit group called the Primary Care Consortium had found out about our application. She invited me to her next board meeting, offering to give me the scoop on the behind-the-scenes reality of health care funding.

If more than one agency from a community applied for the monies, she insisted, that would suggest the community groups couldn't get their act together, and their applications would be rejected. The only way we would all get funding was to submit a joint application, she argued.

"And since your people have already written it, you should just submit it under the name of our more established clinics," she told me.

It didn't make sense to me. Why would I want to do that? The consortium's clinics, which helped poor patients, did not serve the homeless. But somehow she convinced me that the only way Camillus would see any money was to travel the beaten path, the one she said guaranteed funds for all.

It was a mistake to follow her advice. Yes, we got the funds, almost a half million dollars a year—but I'm convinced we would have gotten them anyway. Because we filed under the name of one of their clinics, we had to hand over the control of grant monies to that facility, plus pay an administrative fee. That meant a big fee for minor accounting work. After two years, the relationship grew strained, to say the least. Finally they agreed to return full control of the grant to Camillus.

Like McKinney himself, the grant money was a godsend. It paid for a clinic director, a full-time doctor, nurses, nurses' assistants, and social workers. I remained as the volunteer medical director. The paid positions only guaranteed a skeletal staff to keep pace with the growing number of cases. The volunteers continued to show up in record numbers. And we needed every last one of them. What had begun with five hundred patient visits in the first year had multiplied to over twenty-five thousand, and would eventually peak at fifty thousand visits per year.

My routine began to change as my role expanded. I was no longer simply treating patients and making rounds under the bridge. I was also spending time at the grant-writing desk, in community forums and university lectures, in the despised trenches of the turf wars, trying to educate the educated on homelessness. The changes were inevitable. At times I feared that it was all getting too big, this business of helping homeless people. At times I feared we were losing our original focus—to end a crisis. I feared we might be developing an industry around the problem, instead of making real strides toward finding the solution.

But it all taught me that no matter how big our mission became, how corrupt the health care system became, the real bottom line would never change: If you were poor and sick, you needed more than a prescription.

Yes, the negative elements of the health care arena would always be there. But thankfully, so would the angelic forces. It is no random detail that Camillus's gleaming three-story facility, built with grant money ten years later, would be named the Chichi Greer Clinic.

Ironically, while our growth protected our patients from disease, it made them vulnerable to the epidemic of HMO profiteers, looking for warm bodies to fill their cash-making rosters.

HMOs

and

Other BS

↵

*Alright, we'll leave the homeless alone if
you stop writing your editorials and just
shut up.*

—An official of the Physicians
Corporation of America

A HIGH-LEVEL OFFICIAL OF THE
Miami-based Physicians Corporation of America, one of
south Florida's largest HMOs, was a Southern family doctor who wound up making millions through the magic of
capitation. I remembered the first time I met him, in

1991. He had asked me to come by and see him at his office—he needed a favor.

I found him behind a mammoth desk in his spacious digs, reading. As I got closer to shake his hand, I noticed he had been thumbing through a glossy catalogue—a Learjet catalogue.

I admit, I was strangely amused. Then again, what was I expecting, the *New England Journal of Medicine*?

"I'm trying to decide which jet to buy," he casually remarked.

Here was a top-level official of one of Florida's largest Medicaid recipients, one that was supposed to provide health care for tens of thousands of desperately poor people, wrinkling his brow over the particulars of private jets. But the math was elementary: the fewer patients seen under capitation, the more money available for the Learjet.

In a total non sequitur, he then told me how he wanted to help the poor, which brought us to the purpose of my visit. Dr. Businessman needed a letter of recommendation. He wanted to get his medical license in Florida (he'd relocated from out of state) without having to take the exam. And he wanted my support in this. My letter, he insisted, would allow him to practice medicine in his own clinics. I tried to keep a straight face.

"Well," I offered, "you can always come and observe at our homeless clinic. We don't care if you're not licensed to practice in Florida, you could watch and learn."

"Remember, Pedro, my clinics are all Medicaid HMOs— I have poor people at my own clinics," he quickly reminded me, before launching into a fresh pitch for my help.

I told him I'd think about it. As I left his office, I wondered why this man wanted a Florida license so badly. Was it out of some altruistic desire? Or was it because it was one of the few things this millionaire didn't possess, one of the few things he couldn't buy from a catalogue?

Here was a doctor who hadn't seen a patient in the clinic in God knows how long, and now he was asking me to vouch for his capacity as a physician. I was at a loss to figure out his logic. I mean, what was it? First I'll rip them off, then I'll treat them?

In the end, I agreed to write a letter, but only to say I would supervise him on Tuesday nights at the Camillus Health Concern. He never showed up. ⤳

My arsenal was building. It was time for a counterattack on the HMOs. I fired off op-ed pieces for the *Miami Herald* and *USA Today,* and spoke out publicly to anyone willing to listen. The HMO people hated it, particularly the Learjet guy, who called to protest about one of my opinion pieces.

Our salvos were ringing in the right places. I was invited to Tallahassee to testify before the House Health Care Committee. (Not that our state legislature could be trusted fully to safeguard the poor against health care scams. The former chairman of the Senate Health Committee, a Republican from Miami, now under indictment for Medicare fraud, was fined $5,000 for brokering a multimillion-dollar HMO deal, while still chairman, in which he made $500,000.)

I told state lawmakers how HMOs were stalking poor patients, how their lack of follow-up was costing taxpayers double, first in tax dollars to the HMO, then in public funds at the Jackson Memorial ER. As the hearings proceeded, I watched the HMO people squirm as the horror stories began to surface.

To be fair, I had at one point agreed to become a "primary care" doctor for one of their "products," Family Health, a subsidiary of Physicians Corporation of America, but before long, I saw firsthand how difficult it was for patients—and doctors—to navigate the world of HMOs.

I was treating an elderly patient, an alcoholic, who was battling prostate cancer. He had gone to the HMO urologist, who performed a biopsy, among other things. Both patient and doctor had developed a good rapport. Then, out of the blue, PCA sent a letter to my patient saying he must choose another urologist.

He came to my office crying, reeking of alcohol, and suffering from depression. He said he had called the company various times to request that he be allowed to continue with his original urologist, but no one had returned his calls. He tried several times to reach the medical director, but again, he received no response. I had what I considered to be an urgent medical situation on my hands, since my patient's cancer treatments had been interrupted. Meanwhile, I had to try at least to get him treated for alcoholism.

I picked up the phone and called the HMO's 800 number, asking where I could send this patient for detox. The only place they would approve was clear across town. Couldn't they do better than that? I pressed. No, they said, they couldn't. My anger was building with each dead-end answer they gave me, so by the time I gave up and demanded to talk to the top dog, I was pumped up for battle. He couldn't talk to me, they said; he was in a meeting.

"Put him on the phone."

"I'm sorry, he's in a meeting."

"Put him on the goddamn phone."

At last, the medical director picked up the line. I hit the speakerphone button.

"I have a patient in front of me who has called your HMO, and your office, about ten times, and no one has returned his calls. I have you on speakerphone . . ."

The director was taken aback by my call, angry that I would confront him with one of their "lives" in the room, and as elusive as a snake-oil salesman. The conversation went nowhere and I hung up in frustration and disgust.

Sure, I had given the director a piece of my mind, but it didn't get my patient into detox. I wound up sending him to the county detox center and continued to lobby for his right to see his urologist. At last, the HMO gave in, but the experience left me wondering: How many poor and homeless patients had someone willing to advocate for them? How many had given up these exhausting battles with the HMOs and were settling for substandard medical treatment—or none at all?

My next clash with PCA would unfold against the gentle clinking of crystal, at an American Heart Association gala. A young reporter approached me during the cocktail reception with this message from yet another high-level official of PCA, who was standing across the room: How did I feel about the fact that he was planning to multiply his Medicaid patient rolls? I told her we should pray for the patients.

Later that night, the official came over and asked me why I kept writing my anti-HMO op-ed pieces. He resented my opinion, he said. I explained that freedom is a lovely thing—if he didn't like what I wrote, he didn't have to read it—and let's just say the cocktail-party conversation pretty much deteriorated from there.

"And by the way," I said at one point, "stay away from our AIDS van and homeless clinics."

"Alright, we'll leave the homeless alone if you stop writing your editorials and just shut up."

"It's not just about the homeless! HMOs are screwing the poor in general."

"So," he said calmly, "what will it take for you to shut up?"

It's not easy to stun a Cuban-Irish kid from Miami's Westchester neighborhood, but he did. I smiled and looked him in the eye.

"Okay, I can deal. If you give me world peace, I'll shut up," I said, and bid him a good night. ⤳

Later that night, as Janus and I drove home, I thought about my father, my mentor. I let my mind drift back to some of my earliest memories of him, making rounds in the poorest corners of the north Bahamas, always with honor and respect for his patients. Long before I was a doctor under the bridges of Miami or a med student roaming the Dominican countryside, I learned my first lessons in compassion by watching my father, Dr. Pedro José Greer. I was a young child in the Bahamian islands of Andros and Great Inagua.

My father was the island doctor. And I would watch him in awe as he lovingly practiced the ageless art of healing.

In the morning, my sister Sally and I would go with him in a small rowboat to the outer islands. I remember one particular morning when we traveled with him to an old schoolhouse to vaccinate the children. My father, dressed in his crisp lab coat and toting his black medical bag loaded with syringes and vaccines, docked our rowboat with his distinguished entourage—the boat captain, my sister, and me. He led us through the dense foliage along a dirt path, trekking through the steamy July morning, stopping at a big, one-room whitewashed schoolhouse. Inside, the teacher and students sat on old chairs as a humid breeze filtered through the wide-open windows. The teacher got up to introduce my father.

"This is Dr. Greer and he has come this morning to give us vaccinations," announced the teacher as my father reached down to click open his black bag.

The teacher's words were interrupted by a scramble of children, all jumping up and leaping out the windows. In a flash, the classroom cleared out, leaving us standing in bewildered silence. And then, as if in silent agreement, the grown-ups turned to me, the designated bounty hunter. I recruited my sister with a yank of her arm, and we set out to find the children.

It didn't take us long to spot them in the foliage and

gently coax them back into the schoolhouse. I don't remember exactly what we told them, but they seemed to
trust us, probably because we were children, too. That
morning, all of them got shots—and smiles from my father. It wasn't so bad.

Later, my father would tell me that what Sally and I
had done was all part of the profession—medicine was
about people, about making them feel cared for and comfortable. It was a lesson I took to the States. That, and a
feeling that medicine was the greatest profession in the
world.

We moved to Westchester, or "Weh-cheh-ter," as we
Cubans called it, a neighborhood west of Miami. It was so
far west, on Miami's undeveloped fringes, that if you
drove any farther you'd be in the Everglades. Miles from
the cluttered heart of Little Havana, this was the place exile professionals "moved up" to, a leafy grid of spacious
homes with wide backyards. My father had moved into
private practice, so we could afford the $15,000 for the
house.

The new house was great, a Florida-style structure
sprawled across a quiet canal. Soon our backyard was
bustling with barbecues and impromptu gatherings. One
night, my parents hosted a cocktail party for some rela-
tives and doctor friends. I was helping at the bar, scoop-
ing up ice in plastic cups.

I set a glass down in front of one guest, the grim-faced husband of one of my father's cousins. He was a rich yet reluctant doctor. Out of nowhere, he launched into an assault on his profession. He hated medicine, he said, the sides of his lips curling down in disgust as he spat out unsolicited counsel. Never be a doctor, he said. Do something else with your life—anything else. I stared at him like he was dressed in women's clothes. I had no idea what he was trying to tell me. It was all too heavy and weird for an eight-year-old kid. Besides, fresh in my mind were the scenes of Great Inagua, the schoolchildren trembling behind the shrubs, how they looked at my sister and me, how they eventually followed us back to the schoolhouse. I managed a polite smile and walked away.

I could hear waves of laughter coming from the edge of the lawn, where my father held court. Oh, I thought as I walked toward the group, they must be telling Pepito jokes (naughty Pepito being the Cuban version of Dennis the Menace).

Next to my father stood one of his closest friends from Cuba, a pediatric cardiologist named Dr. Otto Garcia. He told great jokes, even though the previous years hadn't given him much to laugh about. He had spent years in a Cuban jail as a political prisoner. Now in exile, he had just arrived in Florida. A brilliant and well-respected man, he had landed a position on the faculty at the University of Miami School of Medicine.

After the jokes, I stayed to listen to Dr. Garcia's stories of Cuba, tales of prison survival, memories of doctoring in the countryside. His was a true vocation. He spoke of medicine as a thing of beauty, a spiritual calling. He had endured prison by clinging to his dreams of returning to his profession. He vowed to make up for the years he lost in jail. In fact, he said, when he retired from the university, his dream was to treat poor people, for free. Oh, maybe they would pay him in mangoes or chickens, he offered. Maybe he would settle in their village, on some island in the Caribbean.

There it was, so clearly defined for me, the good and the ugly of medicine. One doctor labored with love. The other loved only the perks. You almost could have guessed how their stories would unfold. Today, Dr. Otto Garcia is the pediatrician who cares for the undocumented patients at our clinic at San Juan Bosco Catholic Church in East Little Havana. He lives out his retirement dreams at this two-room clinic in one of Miami's poorest neighborhoods.

The other guy made a ton of money in the HMO business. None of it made him change his mind about medicine.

That I could distinguish between the physician and

the profiteer was a testament to my father's good influence. He had taught me well, I am proud to say. In spite of the noise of the profiteers and the rhetoric of the political BS, my job was simple. I was a physician. I had one responsibility: to care for the patient.

At the time of my struggles with the HMOs, I'd been overseeing the growing Camillus Health Concern for over half a dozen years. I was an assistant dean at the University of Miami Medical School, a former chief resident who had completed two postdoctoral fellowships. But for all that, I had yet to realize one of my great dreams: to work with my father.

It was my sister Sally who brought us together. Chatting with her one day, I wondered aloud why my father had never invited me to join his practice.

My sister shook her head and laughed.

"Why don't you just talk to Dad?" she offered. "Last week he asked me the same thing about you, why his son, an assistant dean, former chief resident, with two fellowships, had not come to work with him."

An obvious breakdown in the CBS—the Cuban Broadcasting System. Going straight to the source, even if that source is your dad, is always a good thing. Days later, I talked to him. Within a month, I left the university and joined his practice. There would be no Learjet catalogues on my desk, but I got to work next to the best doctor I knew. I guess you could say part of me ran away from the HMO nightmares, back to the safe harbor of real, old-time medicine. In the most turbulent times of American health care, it was the only place I felt safe.

And although I didn't know it yet, I would need a safe place to weather the storms that lay ahead.

Getting

Dumped

⌐

Aw, Joe, shut up. . . . You know you're among friends.

—Health care reform
committee member

IT WAS A WEEKDAY AFTERNOON IN
the early 1990s when a taxi dropped off a cardiac patient
in paper surgical greens at the clinic's front door. He had
been discharged from the intensive care unit at a Columbia Corp. hospital in the north part of the county,

nowhere near us. All of a sudden Camillus became the "step-down unit"—in essence, the intermediate facility between intensive care and regular hospital care. The poor homeless man suffered from coronary disease, but still, the hospital did not deem him worthy of admission. Administrators at the Columbia hospital had decided he should be treated as an outpatient—by someone else, of course. They loaded him into a cab and sent him to our clinic. I felt like a jilted lover. They didn't bother to call or write. They didn't even send a message with the patient.

I called them up.

"What the hell are you doing? Camillus isn't a hospital, you know. We're a clinic," I demanded.

My conversations with the hospital's administrator yielded only official rationalizations, fuzz beyond anything I could comprehend. His logic did nothing to raise my awareness, only my anger.

"Since when does your responsibility to a patient end by shoving him into a cab and sending him off to a homeless clinic?"

"Well," the administrator countered dryly, "we stabilized his heart. We met our responsibility."

I figured I must have missed that day in medical ethics class. Finally, we did the only thing we could do: we wrote the hospital a letter saying we would take their patients only after we assessed them at the hospital and made sure the patient's care had not been compromised. In other words, we tried to force the hospital to fulfill its true responsibility to the patient.

By then it was clear: "capitation" had become a euphemism for dumping. It wasn't the first time we got dumped on. Jackson Memorial had refined the art. But when those patients too sick to be discharged showed up in the cab, we just got in and directed the cabbie right back to the ER. And the patient was readmitted. Jackson stopped dumping when we told them we wouldn't take their patients unless Camillus approved the discharge in the first place. It wasn't blackmail, it was just good medicine.

Sometimes it seemed as if the upside-down state of health care had been caused by UFOs or similarly alien entities. After traveling to Washington, D.C., to the belly of the mother ship, I learned that to be true. The first Clinton administration had asked me to take part in its health care reform wave, an invitation that would give me a front-row view of the process and its chief political players.

I had been to Washington in a similar capacity before, briefly, invited by the Bush administration to serve on the 1991 Special Task Force on Minority and Indigent Care, a committee on minorities and health care at the Department of Health and Human Services. I remember the big question at the time was, how do we attract more minority doctors to serve the growing minority populations? Something about that concept didn't sit well with me. Yes, we need more minority doctors. But the implication was, "Bring them in and confine them to the barrio, to the ghetto, to the fringes." Meanwhile, Biff Wellington III, M.D., would have the run of Park Avenue. What minorities really needed, I believed, was access—access to education, access to employment, access to equality.

I have to admit, at times my front-row view showed me more than I wanted to see. It was the early days of the Clinton presidency, which had rolled into D.C. with loads of hope—and a really bad health policy. Actually, as I would soon learn, no real health policy came from the Clinton administration, only cosmetic, reactive gestures. It was all about money. (Remember: it was the economy, stupid.) But initially I accepted the invitation.

I had also participated briefly in the 1992 Transitional Task Force for Health Care Reform, just before President Clinton took the oath. I subsequently declined to be on his health care reform team because it would have meant a move to D.C., which would have interfered with my work in Miami. Besides, no one was talking about health—they were talking about finances. But in 1993 I did agree to serve on the Presidential Health Pro-

fessional Review Group, which consisted of academi-
cians, deans, assistant deans, nurses, and other doctors;
our task was to study the findings of cluster groups ostensibly designing a new policy. That commitment required
my presence in the Old Executive Office Building twice a
week for two months, as opposed to a long-term absence
from Miami.

At first I was caught up in the excitement of the new
administration, but I gradually realized my presence there
would have no impact. I also came to realize that Washington, D.C., was nowhere near America. It existed in its
own surreal orbit, far away from the nation's soul. Policy, I
was to learn, was not about people or their needs, but
about numbers and compromise. Each meeting com-
pounded my feelings of alienation from the so-called reform process. Thankfully, the cumulative effect of so much
frustration was clarity. I was beginning to see where my
journey was taking me. Back home, under the bridges, I
could see only the consequences. But there, in the mother
ship, I could trace the causes. At each meeting, they became more apparent.

Too often the most critical facts never made it to the
discussion table because the seats around the table were
taken up by influence and money. The educated needed
some serious education. How can there be parity and ac-
cessibility if the policies for the poor are designed by the

elite and unenlightened, people with credentials but no understanding of the culture of poverty?

The administration's first mistake was to take me for a representative of the homeless. I was never homeless or elected by the homeless as their spokesman. As their physician, I could only be an advocate. But there were no homeless people sitting at the table. I remember arguing at one of the meetings that managed care for the poor and homeless excluded ancillary services such as transportation, day care, social work. For a poor population, health care had to incorporate more than just medical procedures. "You need social workers, housing, support services," I kept saying. They looked at me as odd man out.

One of the big doctors at the table gave me a dead stare after one of my expositions. "Aw, Joe, shut up," he said. "You know you're among friends."

"If I'm among friends, why can't I bring up these issues?"

And so it went—nowhere.

It became clear the president's senior policy adviser Ira Magaziner was molding a system that didn't make any sense. As time passed, the official, grand discourse about taking care of people was distilled into one about basic policy, about numbers and dollars.

This was the question that seemed to dictate the new

emerging policy: How do you make health care cheaper in America?

Not, How do you make Americans healthier?

We were asked to assess the proposed reforms, but we were expected to do it in the dark. The administration gave us no information, no documents, no data. Nada. But they gave us "guidance," so we wouldn't stray from their mold. I was looking all over the table for that rubber stamp, but they were more sophisticated than that.

Magaziner rattled on about health care in purposely obtuse language, giving us words without substance, delivering messages that required an interplanetary decoder to be understood. One day, I decided that I'd had enough of his alien-speak.

"Sir," I spoke up, "with all due respect, if I really want to know what's going on in this administration, I have to pick up the *Washington Post* in the morning before coming up here. I certainly won't find out by listening to you."

Not even that remark yielded a straight, earthly response.

I was fed up, tired of being lied to and disrespected by the administration. I had given them my time, my expense money, my name, and my reputation. Yet they couldn't give me the courtesy of a straight answer. The whole thing was a setup. It was obvious the cards were stacked in favor of the HMOs and the for-profits. There it was, at last within my sight, the source of the greed and neglect that spread through our communities: it was pouring out of Washington. All the while I'm out there busting my can, trying with all of my strength to hold back the hemorrhage, believing things could change if only policy changed. All the while, I'm wondering when the cavalry folks from D.C. would come. Well, guess what? They ain't coming. They sold out. They ditched the poor long ago.

The entire experience left me feeling hardened and cynical. I realized the system was designed to keep out freethinkers and well-intentioned advocates. People who give a shit could go only so far. The system was designed to harness the mavericks, break their spirit. But I decided it wasn't going to break me, or break my mission. I was just going to do it without them. From then on, I knew in my soul, if we wanted something done, we had to do it with our own hands. We would no longer wait for policy or official responses. The only answers were those we already knew. Only we could make our surroundings better, healthier. I could account only for my own actions, my own diagnoses.

What a journey it had been. I had stumbled into it, young and stupid, horrified that a homeless American would be left to die of tuberculosis. Tuberculosis! As I delved deeper into the abyss, each case overshadowed the one before. In the process, I became known. My face was on TV, my sound bites on radio, my name on too many panels. I plugged away, believing my actions might one day help change the system. But I realized I had been duped.

In a final stroke of absurdity, one Saturday, the review-team directors gave us about four hours to read thousands of pages of policy documents. I never showed up. What was the point? If I wanted science fiction, I could find that back in Miami.

Aliens

in America

~

Today I'm afraid to look the Statue of
Liberty in the eye.
>—Archbishop Edward A. McCarthy

THE GOOD THING ABOUT KNOWING
the cavalry isn't coming is you don't have to wait any
longer. You don't have to expect action from above, official responses or explanations. You have no choice but to
take on the unknown and all the risks such a voyage sug-

gests. The question is, where do you begin? How do you navigate a health care system that locks out the most vulnerable patients? Even the best-connected physician gets stumped by the obstacles all too often, left to figure out the course without a map. Sure, we can prescribe medication for specific ailments, but many times we can't access the true healing elements, the ones that can treat the greater ills in a poor patient's life. And sometimes we simply get there too late.

I have seen this frustration over and over again at the Mercy Hospital clinic for undocumented immigrants at the San Juan Bosco Catholic Church in East Little Havana, a Central American hub just west of Downtown Miami. Manolo Reyes, an executive at Mercy Hospital, and I established that clinic in 1992 out of frustration. At Camillus, I had started to track an increasing number of undocumented immigrants. These patients had nowhere to go. Jackson would charge them exorbitantly, and the community clinics would check for green cards. Not only was Camillus geographically inconvenient for that undocumented population, clustered on the other side of the Miami River in the East Little Havana neighborhood, but it did not have the hospital support for certain lab work and cardiac workups.

While we often sent patients dumped—or potentially dumped—by Jackson to Mercy, a Catholic hospital

on Biscayne Bay in Coconut Grove, we needed to establish a better-coordinated system to serve that population.
Mercy stepped up to the plate and became the first private
hospital in the area to sponsor a $1-per-visit clinic for the
poorest of the working poor. More than 98 percent of the
patients seen there, even today, are undocumented.

I remember one young Nicaraguan woman who ex-
emplified many of our patients there. She complained of
severe digestive problems. After examining her, I could see
why she was in pain: she suffered from a functional disorder of the bowel, a disease that can be gut-wrenching and
debilitating. But her condition was only a symptom of a
greater ailment. I could treat the pains with diet and medication, but I could do little to get her the help she truly
needed to heal.

Here she was, an undocumented woman married to
an abusive alcoholic, a man who often beat her and sexually assaulted her. She feared reporting the abuse because
she had no papers—what if *la migra* caught up with her?
Besides, the only semblance of support she had in this
country was the man who beat her. No wonder she suffered from such an acute digestive disorder. All of her
trauma, all of her insecurity, all of her pain was mani-
fested in her digestive tract.

To alleviate her pain, I gave her some pills and diet
tips—a stopgap remedy. To cure her, I'd have to change

her life. But where could I send her? In the eyes of society she was invisible, just another illegal.

How do you navigate a health care system that has no basic radar to pick up the invisible? Sometimes you have no choice but to become invisible yourself. ⟋

In 1991, I met a patient named Felipe Carrillo, a fifty-four-year-old Cuban refugee who had crossed the Florida Straits on a shrimper on the first day of the 1980 Mariel boatlift. He was a poor farmer from Havana who spent the next decade doing odd construction jobs in California and Miami, working in the labor pools, making just enough money to rent a tiny room in a boardinghouse. After a number of years, he was still working hard to master the delicate balance of life in exile, just barely subsisting, until the day a festering sore in his mouth became unbearable. At first, he didn't tell anyone about the pain—he figured it would go away. Besides, he had no money to see a doctor.

But then the pain got worse, searing into his left cheek.

"I tried to work. But the pain, it was like someone was driving and pounding a knife through my face," he told writer Jacquee Petchel, who documented his struggle in the *Miami Herald.*

The pain forced him to stop working—and caused him to lose his home. He wandered the Mudflats with a green baseball cap on his head and $10 roll of quarters in his pocket. He feared he would die on the street in this strange country, where he had no one. He was desperate when I met him outside the Camillus clinic on a Tuesday night.

On the surface, it was hard to tell the extent of the wound, but it was severe. A large facial tumor had grown from the inside and pierced his left cheek outward. It was already spreading into the roof of his mouth. We treated the wound superficially, called in a social worker, and sent Carrillo to Jackson Memorial for a biopsy.

The labs came back with devastating news: the patient had an inoperable, aggressive cancer that had spread to his lymph nodes.

He would have to undergo daily radiation therapy, not to save his life but merely to make him more comfortable. It was a grueling regimen for any cancer patient, and even more difficult for Carrillo, who had no home, no family in the United States, and no transportation.

Our social worker found him a place to stay in an east Little Havana boarding home. But the other tenants complained about the smell of his tumor. They didn't want him to sit with them at the dinner table. They found the odor of dying tissue too pungent and offensive. They kicked him out two days after he got there.

The social worker found another home, but that one was not much better. After the first round of complaints from fellow boarders, Carrillo picked up and left. He had no energy left to fight for a seat in the living room or a spot at the dinner table.

That same day, one of our other social workers spotted him standing outside the shelter, in the food line that snaked around the corner. We knew he would wind up living on the streets again if we didn't find a way of getting him admitted to the hospital.

But there was nothing in his lab work to justify an admission. The labs were all normal, which makes sense because his cancer was not affecting any major organ. But we couldn't just let him walk out and disappear into the Mudflats again. He was feeble, barely able to eat. If we kept him at the hospital long enough, we could buy social workers time to get him a bed in the county's nursing home for indigents. We just had to stall the system.

First, we needed a reason to keep him—elevated enzymes in the liver, for instance. So we took a quick poll among the interns, and grabbed one who had consumed five or six beers the previous night. I drew the intern's blood and put the results under Carrillo's name. Now we had a cancer patient with elevated enzymes in the liver. Technically, we had a reason to admit him—after all, we had to rule out metastasis to the liver. That bought us three days to get Carrillo into the nursing home, where a government medical van would pick him up and take him to his daily radiation treatments.

Still, I knew we had a patient who didn't want to be there. He wanted to be in Cuba, where he had a son and a daughter. The last time he saw them, the boy was ten, the girl eleven. Now the son was a teacher and the daughter was a nurse. He hadn't spoken to them in years.

"What do I have in this country?" he asked over and over. "I have nothing."

Neither one of us knew it yet, but days after his story was told in the *Herald* and translated in its Spanish-language counterpart, *El Nuevo Herald,* it was picked up by Cuban government TV and broadcast all over the island. His hard-luck, refugee-to-rags tale was easy grist for the Cuban government's propaganda mill. Nevertheless, the regime delivered more than its intended imperialism-bashing propaganda that day—it delivered an urgent bulletin to one particular family, the Carrillos of Havana, Cuba. And it set into motion a frantic drive to bring a lost refugee back home.

Not long after the story aired on Cuban TV, a woman approached my car as I was leaving my office one night.

"Are you Dr. Pedro Joe Greer, the gastroenterologist from Jackson Memorial Hospital?" she asked, carefully reading my name and title from a small handwritten envelope.

"Yes, what can I do for you?"

"As I was leaving the airport at Havana yesterday a lady handed me this letter to give to you," she explained.

It was a letter, written in Spanish, from Felipe Carrillo's daughter in Havana. She had written my name and title just as it had been reported in the *Herald* story. Out of the underground webs of Havana, it was a message for a man who had traveled the underground webs of Miami. Her humble words transported me to Carrillo's old neighborhood, to a place where he was somebody, not simply a statistic in a foreign city's homeless population.

> Most excellent Dr. Pedro Joe Greer:
>
> My name is Ana Maria Carrillo. I am a resident of Havana. I am the daughter of your patient Felipe Carrillo, whom you generously treated at "Jackson Memorial."
>
> Dear Dr. Greer, it had been approximately four or five years that I had no news of my father. But as fate would have it, on June 12, our family here in Cuba learned of his situa-

tion when we watched a television report inspired by an article in *El Nuevo Herald* of Miami, explaining the difficult situation of my father and the honorable, humane, and dignified conduct displayed by you and the social workers at Camillus, who tried to find my father a place to stay.

Our family could never repay you and the others for everything you have done for my father in this act of pure humanity and charity. From Cuba, we are sincerely and eternally grateful.

Dearest doctor, if you have any communication with my father, Felipe Carrillo, please tell them that his daughter and his family are doing everything possible to bring him back home, that we are taking all the necessary steps, that we are awaiting a response from the Central Committee [of the Communist Party].

Please tell him not to despair, tell him to follow all your medical instructions, tell him not to lose hope, to have faith that he soon will return to his family and his home in Cuba. Tell him to take good care of himself.

Tell him his brothers and sisters, Roberto,

Sarah, Tito, and Dianna, send their best, as do
his neighbors and friends here in Cuba . . .

>Most gratefully yours,
>Ana Maria Carrillo
>Havana, Cuba

Thank you very much.

Note: according to *El Nuevo Herald,* he resides
in a nursing home somewhere in Miami.

For all the rejection and humiliation that pounded
Felipe Carrillo in exile, there were multiplied amounts of
love and compassion in his native town. At last, I had before me an authentic backdrop for this man's life, a street
where people spoke his name with affection and nostal-
gia, a room where his photographs still hung, a dinner
table where his place was reserved.

Carrillo wanted nothing more than to be at his family's side. I had long talks with him about his decision to
return. It was the right thing to do, he was convinced, as
was I.

I wrote to the Cuban Interests Section in Washington, D.C., hoping to reunite Carrillo with his family. I got
no response from the Cuban diplomats. So I called them.
But there I encountered a system more cruel and daunt-

ing than the labyrinths of American health care. First they said okay, as long as the patient had a Cuban passport or birth certificate. Encouraged by the news, I went back to Felipe, who quickly shattered my mood.

"How can I give them my passport of birth certificate when those those sons of bitches confiscated all of our documents at the port of Mariel?" he demanded angrily, as if reliving the very reasons why he left Cuba.

So I went back to the Cubans with his reply. Well, they suggested mockingly, why doesn't he just ask someone in Cuba to send them back to him?

"But you took them when he left the country," I stressed. "They're in your possession."

After a few more tense rounds, the Cuban government came to the table, kicking and screaming, and laid down its conditions: we had to guarantee that Carrillo, a Cuban native whose entire family dwelled on the island, would not cost the Fidel Castro government a single peso in medical care. (Behold a man invisible in two worlds.)

That wasn't a difficult condition to meet—he was simply going home to die. Apart from whatever support services we could provide, we couldn't do anything to cure him. At last, the Cuban government relented and Carrillo was allowed to go home. He boarded a Havana-bound flight much like the way he had boarded that shrimper eleven years earlier—with no possessions and no money. And then he disappeared to the other side.

He left Miami not much different than he had found it. Back in 1980, when he landed in south Florida, he saw temporary tent cities set up for newly arrived refugees. More than a decade later, there were other kinds of encampments, where refugees like himself dwelled with refugees from America—refugees like Giles Woodson.

Giles was a fiercely independent fellow, a fixture on the corner of Northwest Tenth Avenue and Twenty-first Street, where he lived for nearly a decade upon a tattered yellow sofa, subsisting on food brought to him by members of the Inner City Ministry of the Miami Temple of Seventh Day Adventists.

I met him in 1991, on a day when I was touring the Mudflats with my friend Paul Mason, the ABC News producer who'd spoken at the PW-GAS forum and who now teaches at Berkeley. Paul wanted to do a story about our medical students' work with the homeless. So one Tuesday in the late afternoon, we drove out to the bridges, the med students and I in my Jeep, and Paul and his crew in a white ABC News van. I walked ahead of the others to ask the residents if it was okay to bring in the TV crew. As I wove through the litter and crack boxes, I expected this would be a routine visit—that is, one that would hold some kind of surprise. Then, out of the corner of my eye,

I caught a glimpse of Ice running toward me with a sense of urgency.

I turned to greet him. "Hey, Ice, what's going on?"

"Doc," he panted as he slowed down, "there's a really sick guy at Tenth and Twentieth."

"What's wrong with him?" I asked.

"I don't know, but you gotta go to him," he pleaded. "He's in bad shape."

Ice, the poor young hustler destined for a life on the streets, had a deep sense of compassion and loyalty to the people of the Mudflats. So, on his advice, the entire party—the network producer and crew, the four students, and I—piled back into our cars and headed toward Northwest Tenth Avenue and Twentieth Street. We circled the block and found the sick man one street over, on Twenty-first, slumped on an old yellow sofa.

Giles Woodson was living on top of a heap of empty wine bottles and garbage. His hair was matted down and filthy, his teeth were missing, and his clothes were so soiled that they no longer offered protection from the elements. He rambled in a delusional stream.

"Just flew in from Georgia. Leaving again in the morning," he muttered nonsensically.

We learned from neighbors that he hadn't moved in weeks, that he couldn't even walk. I cleared the wine bottles from the front of his couch and asked Giles if I could examine his leg. He nodded and pointed to his foot. I snapped on a pair of gloves and gently removed his right shoe. It was so battered, I was afraid it would come off in pieces. The smell of infection rivaled the stench of decaying trash. The students, huddled around me, covered their mouths. Giles wore no socks. A thick film of pus stretched out in a band across the bottom of his foot—it oozed from an infection rooted in his bones. He had no toes—he had lost them to leprosy.

I stood up, peeled off my gloves, and put one hand on his shoulder.

"Mr. Woodson, I think it would be a really good idea if you let us take you to the hospital," I told him.

"No, Doc, that's okay. I'm going to Georgia tomorrow."

We went round and round in this vein for a good ten minutes, and I could tell this was a tough one. Here was a homeless leper with a severe infection of the bones, drunk and delusional and unwilling to accept help. I stepped away and gathered the students, who had never encountered a situation like this one. Most of our patients, no matter how far gone, usually accepted our help. It was painfully clear to me that the only way to save this man's life was to take away his independence and admit him by force under the Baker Act, a Florida state law that allows a doctor to hospitalize an individual for forty-eight hours if the doctor deems that person a risk to himself or to others. Clearly, Mr. Woodson was endangering his own life, but still this wasn't an easy task to carry out.

I went to a nearby pay phone and dialed 911. Within minutes, Miami Fire Rescue paramedics drove up to the corner, put Giles on a stretcher, and took him to Jackson. He was admitted for treatment and declared a ward of the state, then transferred to a nursing home.

It was one of those mixed victories. A life might be saved; a sick man's pain might be lessened. It should have been enough to compensate for taking away his freedom. It should have been enough to smooth the angst of a doctor's decision, to clear the fragments of guilt that sometimes linger the morning after.

Yet this case came back to haunt me one morning seven months later. It turned out Giles Woodson had wandered away from the nursing home and returned to his corner. I gasped as I read the story, in the *Miami Herald's* local section.

HOMELESS MAN DIES
AFTER BEING SET AFIRE

A homeless man sleeping on a street-corner couch was doused with a flammable liquid and set on fire Thursday morning.

Giles Woodson, 59, died hours later at Jackson Memorial Hospital.

Neighbors who heard his screams called paramedics to Northwest 10th Avenue and 21st St. When Miami homicide detectives got to the scene, the killer was gone.

"The couch was still smoldering," detective Jose Granado said. "Everything he had was burnt."

The attack occurred at 2:30 A.M. at the corner where Woodson slept most nights.

Woodson had lived in the area for about 10 years, Granado said.

The homeless man was burned so badly he could barely speak. He could not identify the murderer. Witnesses told police they didn't see anyone near his couch.

I felt as if someone had punched me in the gut. Who could have committed such a barbarity? The overall hopelessness of the case overwhelmed me. Months earlier, I could pick up a phone and get a man committed. Now all I could do was attend the memorial service held at his corner. ⌐

*　　　*　　　*

Giles's murder, unsolved to this day, outraged and galvanized the community. His tragic death put a face on an otherwise anonymous population in a city that continued to feel the consequences of the stagnating social-policy warp, national and local.

In the wake of Giles's death, it seemed as if a new consciousness was emerging regarding the poor and homeless of Miami. At the forefront of this growing community awareness stood Miami's archbishop, Edward A. McCarthy. Concerned about the rising numbers of people living on the street, he invited me to his home one day. He had a lot of questions. What was the extent of this problem? What were the conditions like? What more could the archdiocese do?

I described what I believed was a medical and social emergency. He wanted a tour, so we climbed into my Jeep and headed for the Mudflats. After Archbishop McCarthy took in the sights, he was ready to take action and set off alarms all across town. Several days later, amid the squalor, flanked by public and religious leaders, the seventy-three-year-old archbishop held a press conference and issued a plea for a state of emergency. This is the same archbishop who would be booed by some residents at a Miami City Commission meeting a couple of years later when he spoke in favor of building a new 350-bed homeless shelter in Downtown. He was Miami's gentle apostle, a man who had cleared many paths into the neglected and misunderstood corners of his archdiocese. He had opened up the altar to laypeople. When he took over for the late Archbishop Coleman Carroll, he sold the prelate's walled-in mansion to the deposed dictator of Nicaragua, Anastasio Somoza. McCarthy wanted to break the archdiocese's ties to needless opulence, and he used part of the profits to build a nursing home and moved himself into a modest concrete-block home. This is the man who once spent Christmas with the Haitian refugees held at the Krome Avenue immigration detention center, and afterward declared, "Today I'm afraid to look the Statue of Liberty in the eye."

As it turns out, the archbishop wasn't the only influential figure who sat up and took notice—and action—and pushed for more change. The momentum, it seemed, swept clear across town, right into the chambers of the Metro-Dade Commission, the county's official governing body. A young, energetic commissioner from Hialeah named Alex Penelas, the man who later would be the county's executive mayor, in 1993, had just lost his bid to head the commission. The newly picked commission chief, Penelas's political rival, threw him a murky assignment, a task that seemed all but impossible, well beyond repair: go figure out a homeless-assistance plan.

But not only was Penelas young and hungry, he

was also all too familiar with the topic. Unbeknownst to Penelas's colleagues, his own brother was homeless. The commissioner took on the project with an energy and sense of urgency rarely seen at County Hall. His drive became about more than getting people off the street. It became about establishing a whole new system of care. He mobilized Miami's civic leadership—corporate types, social service veterans, religious figures.

The new wind began to take on gale-force speed. In spite of an often tense process that included the usual politicking and hallway backbiting, a fragile consensus was reached. The newly designed system would be hailed nationally as a comprehensive, progressive response to the homelessness epidemic. It was more than a plan offering food and shelter; it was a system that incorporated counseling, job training, health care, day care, concrete steps to rebuilding broken lives.

The Dade County Homeless Trust was formed to carry out the wide-reaching plan and take charge of the county's homeless services. Penelas and other Dade officials effectively lobbied state lawmakers in Tallahassee to pass the nation's first tax to support the homeless, a countrywide food and beverage tax that now generates some $6 million a year.

Three major homeless assistance centers, or HACs, were planned across the county. To operate them, the private Community Partnership for the Homeless was created. In spite of a citywide uproar, an all-inclusive center went up in Overtown. The bright, airy complex became a virtual small town for people in transition.

But twenty months after it opened, a scandal brought flashbacks of all of our Big Brother nightmares. The center's private leadership began reporting the names of undocumented immigrants to the U.S. government. This policy caused all hell to break loose and brought an avalanche of protest from homeless advocates, Catholic church leaders, and state welfare officials. A group of immigration lawyers who worked with shelter residents withdrew its volunteer services in protest.

Not only that, but the policy completely baffled the U.S. Immigration and Naturalization Service, which doesn't require shelters to report the undocumented. The policy was ludicrous and inhumane. It was the first public sign of culture clash between the partnership's corporate heads and advocates for the poor and homeless.

The entire episode was one of the most divisive chapters I had witnessed in the homeless arena. In the gross overreaction, criminal lawyers were summoned to handle basic immigration matters. Mud flew. The whole affair began to smell of "just business."

Luckily, in the mounting heat of protest, the Community Partnership leaders backed off and tabled the policy. In the larger mission, the illegal-alien policy became a glitch of history, a sad little detour on a noble course.

Even so, it was impossible to deny a new wind was gusting through town, bringing positive change. Four years after the ACLU filed suit against the city of Miami, U.S. district judge C. Clyde Atkins handed down a landmark ruling—the city had violated the Constitution. He mandated "safe zones" for the homeless, places where they could carry on their basic survival activities without fear of arrest. Like a bolt from heaven, Atkins, one of the most humanitarian forces on the federal bench, laid down the law. At last, there would be sanctuary amid daily desperation.

Stood up by the cavalry, Miami's urban soldiers pressed ahead.

Winds

of Change

You can't reason with hurricane season.

—Jimmy Buffett

JUST WHEN YOU THINK IT'S SAFE TO declare small victories, Mother Nature strikes and tosses out all the rules.

Always hurricane-ready, Miami knew the drill. Stock up on batteries and bottled water. Board and tape up the windows. Bring in the pets. And then, hours into your hurricane-watch party, turn on the TV and watch the storm take another route.

But this was no drill. Hurricane Andrew hit after midnight. At 4 A.M. on August 24, 1992, with the winds screeching outside, the burglar alarm sounded throughout our house. The electricity had failed. Outside, the wind howled and sucked. Windows crashed. Trees cracked and thundered to the ground. The noise was like nothing I had heard before. It was relentless, and only getting worse. And so was our fear. We all huddled in my son's bedroom: Janus, seven-year-old Alana, four-year-old Joey, our dog, Blackie, our cat, Ebony, and I. Joey's room was in the center of the house—we figured it was the only safe place to weather the weather. We heard the sound of shattering glass as the window in Alana's bedroom blew out. If another window blew, we would have a powerful wind tunnel in the house. The noise was deafening. Branches and loose metal scraped against the house. Janus and I prayed the other windows would hold, and somehow managed to make the children feel safe. I held Alana close to me and cheerfully told her story after story. None were needed for little Joey, who slept right through the whole ordeal. Later, I would have to explain what happened to the front yard, to the neighborhood, to the city.

We spent the rest of the night in Joey's room. At 6:30 A.M., the phone rang—the most pleasant sound we had heard in hours. My friend Paul Mason, the ABC News producer, was calling from Ohio, asking if we were okay. He had heard that Coral Gables, where we lived, had been hit hardest by the hurricane. That turned out to be less than accurate. We were pounded big-time, but not nearly as heard as areas to the south.

My family and I had survived Andrew. But what about the homeless? Their notice of the hurricane came in the form of police cruisers with bullhorns, announcing the impending storm and orders to evacuate. The rest of us had two days of constant broadcast warnings from smooth meteorologists—the homeless had last-minute orders from Officer Friendly, their pals from court.

Luckily, God spared the homeless. The irony, however, was that in the same stroke of nature, there were suddenly two hundred thousand more.

Although the poorest of the city were spared, the poorest of the southern reaches of the county weren't. The migrant farmworkers took the brunt of the storm. That day I would see the damage for myself.

I looked out the front-door window and surveyed the calm eeriness of the scene outside. Trees and telephone poles were down everywhere. Gone were my mango tree, my oak tree, my ficus. Nothing moved. I wondered whether it was the eye of the storm or it was finally over. I ventured outside and gazed down the venerable streets of my quiet neighborhood. Once a virtual woodland of old Florida trees, our neighborhood looked like the enchanted forest on LSD. I turned to look at my home. It looked like it had been hit by a bomb—tiles blown off the roof, windows punched out, trees all over the place.

Good morning, Miami. Is it this bad everywhere? I allowed myself a few moments of self-pity. But I would have spared the tiny violins had I known what the rest of the devastation zone looked like.

A foreign landscape came into view as I drove south on Florida's Turnpike, the same road I had traveled for decades en route to the Keys. But now, where were the signs? Where were the landmarks? Where were all the trees?

"Hey, Daddy, it's not so bad," chirped Alana, bouncing in the passenger seat of our Jeep, "we don't have to pay tolls today!"

That was because even the toll booths (it seemed as I drove through their remains) had gone the way of the wind. I was driving south, where the worst of the devastation had taken place, because my friend Harve Mogul, president of Miami's United Way, had called from the scene and suggested I help coordinate health care for the hurricane victims. He was asking me to venture into an area entirely foreign to me. Still bleary from the hellish night, I'd jumped in the Jeep, toured the area, and said yes—all my questions didn't come till later.

Mother Nature had turned up the drama and rearranged the plot. And it wasn't long before Mother Politics added her own twists. In the immediate aftermath of the storm, the county's relief effort nearly collapsed as government agencies feuded and politicians bickered. County officials blamed the feds. The feds blamed the state. Meanwhile, conditions in South Dade grew more critical by the hour. There we were, nearly paralyzed by what was being called the most destructive natural disaster in U.S. history. Exasperated, the county's emergency director, Kate Hale, issued an angry and tearful plea that would become Andrew's call to arms. "Where the hell is the cavalry on this one?" she demanded, echoing all our frustrations.

I'd seen plenty on my drive with Alana, and now, I had been calling the Florida Department of Health and Rehabilitative Services for three days to offer help. I had a brigade of physicians, med students, and nurses ready to go. We had vans, medication, portable equipment. But nobody was calling me back. They were all in meetings. We went ahead without them.

A group of us met at Homestead City Hall, about a

thirty-five-minute drive south of Miami, and discussed our emergency strategy. It was decided, at my insistence, that we take care of the migrants in their camps, since they were the poorest.

I got in a van and wound up in the South Dade labor camp. There I surveyed the devastation, superimposed on some of the poorest living conditions I had ever seen in south Florida. The storm had blown away many roofs, but most strikingly it had blown away the figurative roof that had long hidden South Dade's rural poverty. Now that lay exposed for the world to see.

When we got there, one of the camp leaders became our guide. She led us through the clutter of trailers to a half-demolished building at the entrance of the camp. The building, with a fallen palm tree out front, would become our clinic. The palm tree would become our waiting room. The clinic would have to be ready to go by the following morning.

We did what we could for the day and returned to Camillus, where our conference room became our war room. My army of doctors, nurses, and students were equipped and ready to hit the trenches. We hung an area map of Homestead and Florida City and chose three sites to set up our makeshift clinics.

The next morning, the medical students and I led a caravan back south. The team was divided: Two students were in charge of cleaning up the half-demolished building at the labor camp. Two teams were dispatched door to door, to each little shack, to tell the residents about the clinic.

We started seeing patients right away. Ostensibly we were there to treat storm-related emergencies, but like the patients we treated at Camillus, the migrants—the majority of them Mexican-American, Central American, and Haitian—came in with mostly preventable diseases. We were treating once again the lingering consequences of poverty rather than the impact of the hurricane.

The migrants had survived the hurricane pretty well, but that didn't mean their lives were any better. They were still near-slaves in a transient subculture. And yet, amid the extreme heat and humidity and shortages, they would come to us and offer us cool drinks from their donated water bottles, or whatever else they thought we needed. I remember a little canal running along the back of the camp where migrant mothers would bathe their children and dress them up in their best clothes before bringing them into the clinic.

A few days into our stay, one of the army medics on the scene brought me a boy with a nasty gash on his head. She came in carrying the child, followed by the boy's crying mother. We placed the child on the rudimentary exam table. I washed his hairline and carefully shaved it. I had no anesthesia, so I took a plastic bag of ice and pressed it to the wound to numb it. I sutured the gash and dressed it. The boy screamed hysterically with every stitch of my needle. Maria Garza, a friend and longtime migrant advocate, looked at me with a empathetic smile and said, "I think the kid really loves you, Joe."

I shook my head. "No, the kid hates me," I told her. "I just stuck a needle in his head. The mom, she might like me."

Back in the city, my father kept our practice going while I devoted my time to the clinics in South Dade for at least two weeks. That fifteen-day start-up would grow into a three-year commitment for our medical staff. Those clinics stayed open until 1995, when we turned them over to the local community clinic, which was eventually taken over by Jackson.

From where I stood, I could see a diverse community finally coming together. The outpouring of generosity was an amazing thing to witness. People from all over caravaned south with jugs of water, diapers, clothing, and canned goods. People offered shelter to the newly homeless. They offered their time, their labor, and their empathy. This was the true cavalry, people who didn't wait for official action or permission to make a difference. They simply took control. And in the process, they transformed their city. Miami learned that natural disasters bring with them a unifying force more powerful than their destruction. In fact, I learned that the only thing more unifying to a group of Miamians than a hurricane is the fear that a homeless clinic might move into their neighborhood. ⌁

While we were busy dispensing medical treatment, a married couple from my old Westchester neighborhood had started their own relief efforts, distributing food, clothing, ice, and water in South Dade. Gloria and Emilio Estefan were among the first south Floridians to roll up their sleeves and help with the fallout from Andrew. Their efforts would culminate in a megaconcert to raise money for hurricane victims. They opened their hotel on South Beach as the central headquarters for the big event and recruited me, along with Comic Relief's Bob Zmuda, whose organization had already given a half-million dollars to Camillus in the last six years, and Janet Robbie, daughter of the late Miami Dolphins owner Joe Robbie (she now ran Joe Robbie Stadium), to put together the all-star show Hurricane Relief.

I hadn't seen Gloria since the twelfth grade. She went to Lourdes Academy, the sister school to my alma mater, Columbus High. But in spite of her stardom, she greeted me as if the years had not passed.

"Oh, I heard you married Janus," she said casually, recalling her old schoolmate, the captain of the Lourdes cheerleading squad. I quickly realized she was the same old Gloria, the quiet girl we had admired from afar. Before long, our planning sessions took on the feel of the old neighborhood, with bursts of energy punctuated with Spanglish and Cuban coffee breaks.

We had simple but firm rules for the concert.

Rule number 1: No politicians. We turned away senators, our governor, and even some presidential candidate from Arkansas who wanted to play the saxophone.

Rule number 2: No blurred finances. We had to know where the money would go before it was even raised.

Rule number 3: No hidden fees. We decided every last cent would be distributed to the needy. No funds would go to buildings, only to people. No funds would go to the usual administration costs. We got a promise from Harve Mogul of the United Way, which oversaw the distribution of funds. And he kept his word.

The benefit concert raised about $3 million, of which 100 percent went to health and social services for South Dade hurricane victims. The hurricane that tore the city apart brought together a new community, kindred spirits in *la lucha*, the daily struggles, old friends who would become dear ones. God works in amazing ways. Even when policy fails and politicians vanish, miracles can happen. It had taken me years to realize the power that lay in our hands, as individuals and as communities. For so long I had believed the system could change only by decree. But I was wrong. The most powerful kind of change begins on the ground, an impatient wind stirring in otherwise stagnant corners, shaking up the status quo, uprooting old foundations in its gradual, upward sweep.

Social change doesn't come the way hurricanes do, all at once. It can take decades, require great foresight, vision beyond the barriers. It took us more than a decade to build a new clinic for Camillus. And, still, it seemed to bring us no closer to a true solution.

Postgraduate

Lessons

It's for my brothers.

—Homeless boy, age six

I<small>N</small> 1998, <small>AFTER SO MANY STRUGGLES</small>
of the street and against the system, the Camillus Health
Concern landed in a gleaming eighteen-thousand-square-
foot clinic in Overtown. Who would have guessed?

Back in the days when we were treating patients in

the shelter cafeteria, about a mile and a half from this new location, nothing like this seemed possible. Back then, I believed the rash of homelessness was a temporary problem, one that could be hit head-on, patched up, and taken care of within a short time. But fourteen years later, a new, handsome three-story clinic, named for my sister Chichi, stands at the edge of I-95.

It stands, however, not as a monument to our progress as a society—it stands as a monument to our shortcomings. How can one have pride in a shiny new homeless clinic? My sense of pride comes only from knowing our poor patients are now afforded the same comfort and environment as those who can fly to the Mayo Clinic.

A successful homeless clinic, now tripled in space, meant only that we had failed. Each wave of cases only underscored our inability to break the cycle. The number of homeless people continued to increase and we continued to care for them. But not even the county plan that assisted so many who lived in the streets could stop new people from facing the streets. And all our efforts didn't seem to slow the increase of women and children in the ranks of our patients. Even after all our labor, we still found ourselves looking into the eyes of little children and wondering what it must be like to have no home, to find no real solace after a hard day at school.

Sure, everyone was patting our backs for our work, but ours was still "the clinic for those poor people." Still, with each daily wave of patients came the lessons, the gentle refresher courses in reality and humility.

One afternoon, at around lunchtime, I walked into the clinic with a sandwich. I greeted the patients in the waiting room and walked over to the pediatric area, where I found a mother with three of her children. They told me they had come in from the Salvation Army shelter. Her youngest child caught my eye. He was six years old, a little boy with a sweet smile. I offered him my bag lunch, which he graciously accepted. He took the sandwich out of the bag and split it in half. He took two bites out of one half and slipped both parts back into the bag. Then he carefully folded the bag and put it in his pocket.

"Why did you do that?" I asked him.

His reply stunned me.

"It's for my brothers," he said. He was hungry, but he knew his brothers were just as hungry.

God has allowed me to study medicine, to explore the depths of disease and its treatment. He has given me brilliant professors and inspiring mentors. He has opened the tomes of healing, placed in my hands the most precise instruments of modern technology.

And on any random afternoon, he has extended the

most remarkable postgraduate opportunities. He has allowed me to find him in a gentle lull in the city of Miami, under a bridge, in an emergency room, in the waiting room of a neighborhood clinic, in the wisdom and humanity of a homeless child.

The goodness of that child has stayed with me through the years. I have often asked myself: Could the lesson of his generosity be multiplied by a community, a government, an entire nation? Could such a spirit help mend a broken system?

Could we look at a disheveled man or woman on the street and withhold judgment?

It was a Tuesday night at the clinic when a young woman in a tattered red dress came in. She was about twenty-five years old, but she seemed a lot older, the lines of her battle-weary face barely concealed beneath a smudge of stale makeup. Her soiled clothes, a swath of spandex, told the story of her hard life on the streets. Her eyes revealed her turmoil. Whatever her story, she deserved a bath and rest.

That night, I was working with the third- and fourth-year medical students. I sent Carlos, a third-year student, into exam room 2, where she sat weeping.

Within minutes, the student rushed out of the exam room.

"Dr. Greer," Carlos called to me in a hurried tone. "I

can't get a history out of her. I don't know what to do."

"What's the problem?"

"I don't know. She's crying like a baby. I can't get her to talk to me," Carlos replied.

"What's your guess? Emotional? Physical? Drugs?" I insisted, giving him a signal to follow me.

"I don't know," he repeated more urgently as we walked toward the exam room. "The chart says she's been here once before. Some dermatologic condition. No history of psychological problems noted then. Does smoke some crack. The perks of prostitution."

I stepped into the exam room and found a desperate woman. She was trembling. I extended my hand to greet her.

"We're here to help you. Do you hurt somewhere?" I asked, gently nudging her elbow to give her sense of stability. She was full of tears, gasping for air.

"It hurts down here," she said between sobs, holding her lower abdomen and doubling over. "It feels like it's burning. It won't stop. Please help me, please."

We let her calm down a bit before we examined her. As I palpated her tender belly and examined her further, I concluded that her symptoms and the exam suggested a mix of pelvic inflammatory disease and other sexually transmitted diseases.

"It'll be okay," I told her, trying to offer a little reassurance. Slowly she began to tell us why she had really come to the clinic, when she could have gone to the gynecologists at the public health unit.

"I was raped, raped hard last night," she said, as she doubled over again in tears and shame.

"Why didn't you go to the Rape Treatment Center at Jackson last night?" I asked. After all, it was just a couple of miles away, a top-notch center.

"Doctor," she said with a look that suggested I should know the answer to my own question. "Look at me. Look at how I'm dressed."

She paused and then again broke into sobs. "I couldn't take the comments people make."

She was right. The mammoth system of health care could offer excellent medical care and all of the best technology. But it could offer no solace, no empathy, no protection from prejudice. That's because there was a gaping error in its construction—its heart was left out. No matter how advanced, the system lacked what that young woman needed that day—compassion.

What possible lessons could we as a society learn from a homeless hooker? Plenty. We can learn to listen. We can learn to ask the right questions.

Long ago, the course of American health care was defined by all the wrong questions, economic questions. Therefore, we should not be surprised that we were left out of the answers. Policy will be about us only when it is designed by us. And that will happen only when we take it as a meal to be shared with a brother or sister who is hungry.

Peace.

Acknowledgments

⌒

I HAVE BEEN ABLE TO TELL MY STORY, practice medicine, live life to its fullest because I have had my friend, my wife, my partner, Janus, with me. Thank you for everything, I love you. My two kids, Alana and Joey—the world is yours to make better; you've made mine better. I love you both. Mom and Dad, you guys started it. *Gracias, te quiero.*

Liz Balmaseda, for being my friend and such a great writer. We did it. Becky Cabaza, I've only had one editor in my life, and I was lucky enough to get the best. Thank you for your guidance and patience. I hope I got a good grade. Raul Mateu, my friend, agent, and fellow Gator, thank you for the belief you had in this book, then making it happen.

The Brothers of the Good Shepherd, for so kindly doing God's work, thank you. To the Marist Brothers, for teaching us how and why to do the right thing. To the Sisters of Saint Joseph of Saint Augustine, Mercy Hospital, for teaching us as children, then as physicians, thank you for making Mercy, a hospital with the right mission: to care for the patient.

To my mentors and peers who taught me more than medicine—you've all taught me how to be a physician—Pedro José Greer Sr., Mark Gelbard, Eliseo Perez-Stable, Eugene Schiff, Tino Castellanos, Otto Garcia, Arvey Rogers, J. Maxwell McKenzie, Fernando Calmet, Bernie Fogel, Mark O'Connell, Lawrence Gardner, Danny Castellanos, Rafael Llanso, John Drawbert, Manny Carbonell, Franz Stewart, and Warren Quillian. Some of you taught me directly, all of you by example. Thank you for making life better for people and then teaching us how to do it. Jim O'Connell, medicine's real saint. Phil Brickner, the man who started it all, then showed us how. James Reuler, for getting me started. Rafael Mas, my physician, who has never refused a patient. David Lawrence, my dear friend, for doing what is right. Roger Soman, for always being there.

Thanks to all who have made Camillus and Saint John Bosco Clinics what they are today. I specially want to thank Alina Perez-Stable, Terisa James, Ross Collazo, Manolo Reyes, Jim Shultz, Donna Reno, and Fran Esposito: you all have made people's lives nicer. Doug Molloy, my old roommate, thanks for driving down weekly to help the homeless; you still owe me a suit. David Glickman, you put on our first fund-raiser, which built the clinic and eleven years later you're still doing it. Benjamin Waxman, you led the fight against Goliath and made the homeless feel like David. Sergio Gonzalez, thanks for your ethics, morals, and bringing everyone to the table. Carlos Santeiro, class of 1974, we did OK, thank you for everything.

Julio Ruiz, Bob and Beth Sackstien, Meg Laughlin, Tom and Bill Harrington, thanks for your hearts and minds. Andy Menendez, may God bless your soul; you cared when nobody else did.

Tito, you taught me the dangers of altitude.

Paul Mason, my fellow MSI member, now you teach what you have mastered. Thank you. Bob Curvin, thank you for your presence. Caroline Thompson, you do so much good for those who need it most. God bless you. Bob Zmuda, you created a way to support the poorest in America and still made us laugh. Dennis Albaugh, thanks, we still need hippies. To everybody at Comic Relief and HBO who make it happen. Thanks, Pat Connor. Paul Rodriguez, only your heart is larger than the brilliance of your humor. Thanks for visiting the clinic and the patients. Whoopi Goldberg—God bless your passion and intellect to make the world better.

Al Durruthy and Diana Gonzalez, thanks for covering the plight of the homeless when nobody else did. I'd like to thank the *Miami Herald, Diario Las Américas,* ABC,

Acknowledgments

✢ 2 0 2 ✢

NBC, CBS, PBS, Univisión, Telemundo, and all the news agencies who have portrayed our story and the story of the homeless with dignity and fairness.

Gloria and Emilio, you know why I thank you. *Gracias.*

Thank you to all who have made Camillus House work; we have given the poor a hand and Miami a soul.

Finally, to every person who has had the privilege of treating the sick or the honor of working with the poor: thank you.

About the Authors

Pedro José Greer Jr., M.D., is the award-winning founder and volunteer medical director of Miami's Camillus Health Concern, a health care clinic for the poor and homeless, which serves more than ten thousand men, women, and children annually. The winner of numerous honors, including a MacArthur Foundation "Genius" grant and the President's Service Award in 1997, Dr. Greer has served as an adviser to both the Bush and the Clinton administrations on health care issues. He holds a diverse number of appointments, ranging from serving as a trustee for the RAND corporation to sitting on the board of directors of Comic Relief. In addition, Dr. Greer is a professor of medicine, a gastroenterologist and hepatologist in private practice, and the former Chief of Gastroenterology at Mercy Hospital, a full-service hospital in Miami. The son of Cuban immigrants, he grew up in the Caribbean and in Miami.

Liz Balmaseda is a Pulitzer Prize–winning journalist who writes a regular column for the *Miami Herald*.